We Survived

A True Story of Control and Mental and Physical Abuse

August 28, 2022

Sandra L. Buehring

PAGE PUBLISHING
Conneaut Lake, PA

First originally published by Page Publishing 2023

ISBN 979-8-88793-472-3 (pbk)
ISBN 979-8-88793-520-1 (hc)
ISBN 979-8-88793-495-2 (digital)

Printed in the United States of America

I dedicate this book to the people who helped me escape: my mom and dad, who were always there for me no matter what I did; my sister, who cared for my children so I could work and didn't have to pay for childcare; my brother, who drove me and the children from Oshkosh, Wisconsin, to Tucson, Arizona; my children, who were always there by my side loving me; and the Lord my God, without whom I couldn't have made it!

CONTENTS

FOREWORD

I have written this book to assist men and women in recognizing the symptoms of control and physical and mental abuse. With this knowledge, you can understand how it affects the abused person and where and how to seek help. Also, I want you to know that the abused can do it and should!

At the beginning of a relationship, you are getting to know someone.

It isn't always apparent that a person has an abusive personality. Only later will they show their true character. For me, it became evident shortly after I was married. As soon as I was married, I was trapped and could do little about it without much hurt and expense! In writing this book, I became aware of a few times before marriage when I should have recognized something was wrong.

Abuse starts slowly and advances as time goes on. So don't stay and think, "Things will get better." They will not. They will only get worse. The abuser will promise they will not do it again, but rest assured they always do. And it *will* get worse.

I believe abuse is a learned behavior. In my case, my fiancé's father was an abuser, his grandfather was an abuser, and his great-grandfather was also an abuser. It was their family's "normal." That is what happened in my marriage. Only after my wedding did I and my family realize this.

My family thought I had met a genuinely lovely religious man. After realizing this was wrong, I determined my sons wouldn't continue the pattern. So even though I believed that I still loved the man I initially fell in love with, I realized that I didn't love the man who became my husband and father to my children. Check your feelings and see if this is what has happened to you—you love the person you initially fell in love with, but the one you married is not that person. Be sure this isn't why you are staying in your marriage. I divorced my husband to give my children a chance at a happy life and marriage. Recently, my younger son thanked me for leaving and giving him a chance at a loving family foundation. He never knew his father and what the rest of us went through.

I lived for thirteen years in an abusive relationship. I started divorce proceedings three times. After the first two, he said he would change and wouldn't do it again. Believing him, I stopped the divorce papers twice. Things would go smoothly for a while and then slowly deteriorate again.

My mom and dad were visiting once when I started divorce procedures, and I told them that the kids and I wanted to return with them. When my parents left, my husband convinced me to stay. The third time, I finally realized he wasn't going to change; I got up the courage to leave when I realized that I was setting up my sons for the same relationships with their partners by waiting. Do not wait thirteen years as I did. Every year a child remains in this type of family situation, and they grow to believe it is normal. When I divorced, my children were thirteen, twelve, eight, and one. Only the one-year-old was not affected by the family dynamics. The divorce was worth it and helped all my children find a new "normal" and have better lives and marriages.

It is hard for people to understand why the abused will stay when they should flee. It is a tough decision once you are in the situation. Usually, you don't have money to support yourself and the children, and you have been mentally told many times that you cannot take care of yourself and the children. They will tell you the fights are *your* fault. They are *not*! In many cases, you are brainwashed. If you know someone in such a situation, help them, and please don't judge them. Most people will say, "I don't understand why they don't just leave." It takes walking in the abused person's shoes to understand the consequences, as there are many to realize before you act.

As you read this book, if you start to see some of your actions as abusive, please begin the process of getting help so you can change and be the loving partner that you and your significant other deserve.

If you are jealous of your significant other, remember that they started seeing you because they liked you, and they will "remain" with you if you are a loving and responsible partner. You don't have to beat them to stay, love, or do what you want. If you treat your significant other lovingly, they will "choose" to stay with you. You can change if you have the desire to have a healthy relationship. It does take time and help. Would you please get the help you need for a better life for yourself and your significant other? The goal of this book is to show you that you can get out.

If you find you are being abused, get out and start over. Find someone to help you and begin one step at a time. It would be best to let a trusted family member or friend know your situation first and go from there. I say "trusted" because you need to know that they are on your side and won't repeat secret information to the abuser so they can find you.

I talk about my "rock" at several points throughout the book. My mom is my rock, and I can count on her to be there for me. The abused need to find such a person because they need a support person to help them—someone they can call when they are afraid to do something alone or need to talk. I could always count on my mom to go on a trip, go to a dance, chat with me, or help me out. They will help you safely move forward.

It isn't going to be easy, but you can do it. We did it and left our home and my job to move two thousand miles to start over. I was thirty-one years old with four children depending on me for their lives. We had no home, no job to count on, and little money at the time. My family lived in Tucson and were willing to do anything necessary to help. There was little money, but little by little, we made it and are today a big, wonderful, happy family with many grandchildren and great-grandchildren. You can be a survivor too. Don't be afraid to take that first step.

Have the National Domestic Violence Hotline telephone number (800-799-7233) and the National Sexual Assault Hotline telephone number (800-656-4673) in your possession. I would have these telephone numbers on paper in your purse or wallet. *If you are being abused and find yourself among others, paramedics train you to yell to the people to "call 911" instead of calling help.* People sometimes don't want to become involved if you call for help; however, they will usually respond if someone asks you to call 911. Likewise, if you are in any frightening situation, yell, "Dial 911," so someone will help you. *The Poison Help number is 800-222-1222.*

I have only used my name in the book to protect those who want to remain anonymous. My new husband permitted me to use his name. You will read about Sam later in the book. I have tried to write our story so it doesn't hurt anyone. If my words offend the abuser, I am not responsible for their actions or how the truth in this book might affect them.

As you read this book, you can see that we didn't have an easy time, but we also had some pretty beautiful times and came out with an extraordinary life.

I wish you an extraordinary life!

ACKNOWLEDGMENTS

I want to thank the five people who offered to critique the first draft. A special thanks goes to my daughter-in-law, Robin, for editing the first draft with so much thought, effort, and encouragement.

CHAPTER 1

Childhood

I grew up in a loving, lower-middle-class family. When I was a baby, my father had a feed grinder, and he ground feed for the farmers. He did that for several years. I was too small to remember those days. I remember when my father was a blacksmith and owned his shop. He fixed the equipment for the farmers in the area and even designed a trailer to haul large gas drums for bringing gas to homes for heating. He applied for and received a patent for the product. He worked at the blacksmith shop until his health became so bad that the doctor told him he needed to go to a warmer climate.

My mother packed cookies at the Ripon Cookie Factory in Ripon, Wisconsin. They were allowed to buy the cookies in bulk, and I remember her bringing home five-pound boxes of cookies. The package was big, and it was on the stairsteps going to the upper floor, where our bedrooms were. Sometimes we would sneak cookies on our way to bed. They wanted to promote Mom, but she liked working on the line with the other women. So she said, "No," and continued packing the cookies. One day, one of the women lost her ring. They looked everywhere to see if it was in the cookies but never found the ring. Wonder who did find the ring?

My family had three kids: my sister, the oldest; myself, the middle child; and my brother, the youngest. I was born on March 13, 1941, just before Pearl Harbor. My brother was born on April 13 and is thirteen months younger than me. My mom was so embarrassed to be pregnant again with my brother. She didn't want anyone to know—especially her mom! At the time, women believed you couldn't get pregnant if you were nursing a child. She told us, girls, not to believe that "old wives' tale."

Thirteen is a lucky number in our family as many members were born that day. My youngest son was born on the 13th. Several family members also passed on that day. My sister said, "Well, that isn't a good day then."

And I reassured her, "Yes, it was because they passed into heaven." She had to agree with me. She didn't agree with me very often.

My maternal grandparents lived in Germany, and many family members moved to Russia when that country asked the German people for help learning how to farm. The Russian government gave the German families farmland to encourage them to come, but the Russian people became jealous of this arrangement. My great-grandmother had moved with all the family to live in Russia.

Because life was getting worse and worse in Russia, they decided to move to America. My great-grandmother told the families she could afford to get them all to America but would have no money left to support herself after she arrived. The families agreed to take care of her if she got them all to America. So she paid for all of them to come. I'm sure they all agreed that it was a win-win for everyone. Using all her money to get the family to safety was a very unselfish thing for my great-grandmother to do. You will find in the book a picture of Mom's entire immediate living family. Two of her brothers had passed away when a photographer took the picture.

They came to America through Ellis Island. That is only three generations back, which I thought was very unusual. Usually, people came years before, and you didn't know them. We could see and speak with our grandparents, who were so proud to have come to America. I remember visiting Grandma and Grandpa, and the aunts and uncles lived next door. While they were poor, Grandma always had nickels for us kids when we came so we could go to the store and get an ice cream cone.

One of the families decided to return to Russia and didn't stay in America. The families here would send packages to them to assist them with a better life because it was hard for them in Russia. The families lived along the Volga River, the longest river in Europe.

My heart swells with pride when they televise people getting their American citizenship. To think that these people worked so hard to get here and become citizens makes me a very proud citizen myself. When you realize that they left behind other family members, knowing they would probably never see them again, it is very courageous on their part.

My grandma and grandpa studied hard to become citizens. They needed to speak English well enough to become citizens. However, they returned to speaking German afterward and soon forgot English. They only spoke German at home and with other family members. My sister, my brother, and I could not understand them, which was sad.

My grandma and grandpa lived across the street from the German church. The sermons were in German, and they went to church often. My grandma cleaned houses to earn money so my mom could learn how to play the piano. My mom played the organ in the church and became proficient. She didn't need to read the music as she could play by "ear."

Whenever the minister purchased a new Bible, he would give my grandpa his old Bible. I remember my grandpa always reading the Bible in his favorite chair. All the Bibles were in German. He had many German Bibles, and when he passed, the Bibles were given to family members and finally to me. One of the Bibles is very big and very old.

Most of my uncles were in military service during the war; however, my dad's work was too important, so he didn't serve in the armed forces. My dad had a feed grinding business and ground feed for the farmers. The government believed it was more important for him to stay home and grind feed for the farmers. We all are very proud of and grateful to those men and women who did serve.

My earliest memories as a child are of living in Fisk, Wisconsin. We lived most of our young lives in a two-story home on a small creek that ran through Fisk. The land along the river and our property was rough. Daddy brought in many loads of soil to build up the area, making it level. He added grass to the site and transformed it into a park. It looked beautiful. Our house had four bedrooms—two upstairs and two downstairs—and one and a half baths. In today's world, the half bath would be inside the home. Ours was outside and referred to as an "outhouse." But when necessary, the half bath was convenient! I remember running several times to the "half bath."

It was a joke that you could miss the town if you closed your eyes when you came down the hill through Fisk. Yes, it was that small—maybe a mile or two. It was a straight road. There were no traffic lights and no bank. We did have a grocery store, a blacksmith shop that our dad owned, a small train depot, and a one-room schoolhouse. Approximately eleven families lived in Fisk.

The train stationmaster only had one arm, and all the children feared him because he was different until we learned that he lost his arm in military service. That made a big difference because our uncles were in the service, and we were proud of our uncles. The stationmaster was very friendly to the children, and we grew to like him as a good friend. He always had treats for us or nickels and dimes to get goodies at the store. He had become good friends with my mom and dad and eventually moved to Tucson. When we later moved to Tucson for my dad's health, he helped my mom and dad find a rental home and work. He was a wonderful friend to them. They had already met his wife by this time, and she also became a good friend.

My dad would get milk from the farmer up the road, and my mom would have to pasteurize it because otherwise, we would get sick. The milk provided by the farmer was raw, and we were not used to raw milk, so to us, it tasted terrible. My dad decided to get goats and see if their milk was any better. Mom would milk the goats. She gave us the milk to see if we liked it any better. The answer was a definite "no." Our mom was a good sport. She was a city girl but "believed she could do anything." She set out to milk those goats. As soon as she would get the pail full, the goat would kick the bucket over. We heard some new words growing up because of those goats. I don't think the goats lasted very long.

We always had pets. Mom was afraid of dogs, but she accepted our animals because Daddy loved them. We had guinea pigs, parakeets, kittens, and dogs. Daddy had a red Irish setter named Rex, whom he took hunting. Once, when on a hunting trip, Rex ran away. No matter how and where they looked, they couldn't find him. When they got home without Rex, we were unhappy and scared that Rex would get killed on the road, so we prayed. And lo and behold, someone found Rex and brought him home—a young kid's mind at work. We were so grateful.

We went to school in the one-room schoolhouse through all eight grades. The teacher taught all classes and students in the same room. After finishing my school lesson, I could listen to the other courses and learn ahead. I loved school. A picture of the Fisk School is in the book. My brother is in the photo. The one thing I didn't like was when we received our grades. The teacher weighed us at the back of the room, where everyone could see. She recorded our weights on our report cards. Because I was a heavy little kid, everyone wanted to see how much "Sandy had gained." It was so humiliating. I hope they don't weigh kids like that today.

We didn't have a school library, so the teacher would drive into Oshkosh to the library every four to six weeks and take out many books for us to read. She would come back with all these different kinds of books for all the grades. We would be all over those books. There would be history, science, family, animal, art, and any other books she thought would be good for us. After several weeks, we had to have the books read and returned to her, and she would do it all over again. She knew what kind of books we all liked or should like, and that is what she would get for us. She was one dedicated teacher. One of the best!

At the beginning of the day, she would read a chapter in a book that was too hard for us to read, and we learned to enjoy more challenging texts and books that we usually wouldn't read.

Our teacher was very imaginative. When we were in the lower grades and learning new words, she would draw a ladder on the chalkboard and put the latest words in the openings of the ladder. We would have to repeat the words up the stairs to get a small prize and praise. It was fun to try to get to the top. It took us several days to do it because we learned several new words each day. She also had little cars on a string that she pushed ahead as we learned something new, and if we got to the end of the road, we got a little prize.

Someone reading this book might remember the class over the radio called "Let's Draw." Can you imagine a drawing class where you couldn't see the teacher and still learn to draw? Our teacher thought it was a waste of time, so she would forget when it came on. But I never did because I loved drawing; if I could remember, I always went up to her and reminded her. I took art lessons as an adult, and my art hangs in our home. You will find samples of my artwork in the book.

I was a typical tomboy when I was younger. I loved to play baseball because I could hit that ball! As I said earlier, I was a chubby child, and it went far when my weight met the ball. As a result, everyone wanted me on their team. You can imagine the fun those games were with the children's different ages in grades one through eight.

We played hopscotch, Jacks, and Annie Annie Over at recess and home. Do any of you remember Annie Annie Over? It was a nineteenth-century game when I looked it up on the computer.

We didn't have indoor plumbing at the school and had a "half bath" or an outhouse for a bathroom. I'm speaking of life in the 1950s. I once told my grandchild's class that we used an outhouse for a bathroom; they thought it was hilarious! The teacher would forget she let us out for a bathroom break; especially if we were quiet, she would forget we were outside, and we got extra time. I got in trouble by telling everyone to keep still; we were out there for a long time. Oh, was the teacher mad! I was supposed to "know better."

Arbor Day was a big thing back then. All the children had to rake and clean the schoolyard. Afterward, we would have a massive bond fire with the leaves and branches. We would have food to eat. It was one day each school year, and while everyone didn't like the work, we all pitched in and finished it as fast as possible so we could play and eat. With all the trash around the city, it might be a good idea to start Arbor Day in schools again. I believe the children will clean up our streets because they will "see how horrible the clutter looks."

My brother and I always got into trouble during the summer and after school. And of course, my sister had to help get us out of it. A few dogs in the neighborhood were named Sandy, and when they called the dogs, I always wanted to answer. It wasn't funny to me. I didn't like my name in those days. When I went somewhere, they would ask, "Do you want to be called Sandra or Sandy?" I told them I would go by any name they wanted to use.

We found exciting and fun things to do. Asparagus and berries grew along the railroad tracks. We would walk along the railroad tracks and pick as many berries as possible, and Mom would make berry muffins or have berries over ice cream. The following week, we would walk along the tracks and pick the asparagus. They were so good. You can't get better than "fresh asparagus" and, also, sweet corn on the cob. These are some of the things I miss from Wisconsin.

The creek was usually shallow in the summer, and we could walk across the stones. My brother and I could usually be found down at the stream. We loved to find the tadpoles and catch them. We always threw them back again "so they could grow up to be frogs." Sometimes (usually), we would slip off the slippery rocks, fall in, and get our shoes and socks wet.

Of course, our mom believed the water was dangerous and didn't want us by the water, so we would have to hurry and hang our socks and shoes on the clothesline to dry before she came home from work. We were short and had to enlist my sister to help us reach the clothesline. Our sister always gave us a tongue-lashing, just like a mom. Sometimes the socks and shoes wouldn't be dry when Mom got home. Mom would fake a scolding, and we would promise to be more careful. We would be out again the next day.

Once, we were walking on the stones in the creek, and one "squeaked." We walked over it more than once, and it always squeaked. Well, that was just too much excitement for my brother and me. We had to pick up the stone and see what was making the noise. It was newly born little mice. We were just beside ourselves with excitement. Anything with four legs was a "pet." But these were too young to take home, so there were no new pets that day. Mom would not have agreed to mice as pets! But we were so excited to find them. We put the stone back and left them alone.

A mouse got in the house's back door, and my brother and I chased it all over the hallway, trying to catch it. It would run up our pants legs to get away, and we would scream. We finally got it but had to let it go outside because we couldn't keep it as a pet. But we did try. Mom would have none of that, and our cats would have had a good meal.

Railroad tracks ran through town over the creek and road at a forty-five-degree angle. The tracks cut the village in half, a little more than a half mile on each side of the bridge. The train came through twice a day and had six to ten cars. It was a small train. Sometimes men on little "handcars" would come down the tracks. We would wait for the train whistle twice a day.

When the water in the creek was high, big carp would swim up the river. That always was so exciting because it didn't happen often. We would run to my dad's blacksmith shop and get spears that he had made from pitchforks. We would sit on the railroad ties over the water and spear the fish. Sometimes men would come along and feel we kids didn't "know how to spear the fish," so they would take away our spears. But if we were quiet, they wouldn't know we were there. I prefer to spearfish instead of using a rod and reel. It is much more exciting than watching a bobber!

One year, the carp swam up the creek in such abundance that it was easy to pick them off. The people caught so many that they didn't know what to do with them. Someone told my dad that it would be good fertilizer if he buried them in our garden. No one thought ahead to deal with the smell when they started to rot. Oh my, what a scent! When my grandmother visited, which she often did, she couldn't stand the smell and would stand there retching. Of course, we thought that was funny, but she didn't. She kept telling my dad he had to do something about the smell—and it was too late. The fish was rotting in the garden. We just had to wait for the smell to go away!

Living out in the country, we seldom went to the doctor except for our childhood shots. One year, I got a big bump on the back of my hand, and it moved back and forth when we touched it. It didn't hurt, but it kept growing, so finally, Mom took us to the doctor so he could see what the bump was. The doctor looked at my hand and then at the books on his shelf. Finally, he pulled one off the shelf, and we thought he would look at it to see the diagnosis. It turned out to be a ganglion cyst.

Our mouths flew open when he lifted the book and slapped it down hard on my hand, and the bump disappeared. We didn't know, but he looked for the giant book to break the lump. Mom paid the bill, and we left. It never grew back.

As I sit here writing this book, it is the Fourth of July. The firecrackers are sounding in the night sky. It is beautiful as they go off on "A Mountain" and other small cities surrounding Tucson. There is a big "A" on the mountain, so it is called "A Mountain." You can see fireworks all across the sky.

Muffin, our dog, is scared and curled up next to my husband and me. After surviving the sad days, I was finally able to recognize good qualities in a spouse and ended up with a happy marriage. Thinking of the fireworks, I reminisce about going to Oshkosh, Wisconsin, as a child, sitting on a blanket in the park. We watched the fireworks set off on the island of the Fox River. Those were the only fireworks we could see in those days, which was a big deal for families. It was a relaxing time for the parents, who could have the whole family there.

We had several friends living in Fisk, including one with a young pony. My brother and I would go to their home and ride if she let us. She was born when her parents were older and was an only child. The parents had wanted a child for so long and were excited when they had one. They were willing to do anything to make her happy, so they bought her the pony she wanted. Her parents had to permit us to ride because it was a liability for them, and we understood that. We would take turns. As I was heavy, our friend had to cinch the saddle so it wouldn't slip. One time, it wasn't tight enough. The pony was spooked and took off up the hill, and the saddle slid to the side with me hanging on for dear life.

One of the men at my dad's shop saw me flying up the hill and told my dad that his daughter was on a pony and was slipping off the side. I was caught at the top of the road by someone. Thankfully, they stopped the pony, and I didn't fall off or get hurt. I always loved horses but was afraid to ride unless it was a very mild-mannered horse after that little excursion. Sadly, we weren't allowed to ride the pony after that. We did understand.

Childhood Summers

Money was always short for our family. My mom was a good seamstress and would make clothes for us when we were young. Our aunt and uncle lived on a farm and had lots of animals in those days. The manufacturers deliberately made the feed bags from cotton, which came in pretty colors. When it was time to purchase feed, the women selected several of the same patterns so that they could make clothes out of the bags. My aunt would save several of the same design that she thought were pretty for Mom. We had many beautiful garments made of these "feed bags."

Comic books were a big thing back then. Parents could buy their children subscriptions, which would arrive once a month. It was a big deal when they came in the mail. We would get Bugs Bunny, Archie, Casper, Donald Duck, and Mickey Mouse, to name a few. Mom and Dad had to get three, or there would be a fight about who could read them first. We were quiet the day they came—all reading our comic books. I don't know how Mom and Dad could afford them for us, but they did. They made sure we had books to read, and to this day, we all love to read and made good grades in school. My sister was valedictorian of her high school class. She had to give a speech at the ceremonies. She received a scholarship to college; however, she did not want to continue college after attending the first year. She had her fill of schools. My brother did go on to college and graduate. So later, when I could not continue school, it was an embarrassment.

As a parent, as we raised our children, I would get little books for my children when I got groceries. It made my husband so mad. He thought books were an unnecessary expense. The kids just loved them. They all love to read and have done very well in school.

Sometimes, when school was not in session in the summer, we would get bored and go to the blacksmith shop to ask Daddy if we could ride our bikes to our aunt and uncle's farm and help. It was several miles to their place, but we loved to go and feed the sheep and help put the hay bales on the wagon and anything else a kid could do. We would stay all day and ride home in time for Mom to get home from her work at the cookie factory.

Some days, we would talk among ourselves and decide that Daddy needed an ice cream cone if it was hot out. Because I was the bravest, I always got to be the spokesperson. We would go to the blacksmith shop, kitty-corner from our home, and I would ask Daddy, "Would you like an ice cream cone?"

Of course, Daddy always said, "Yes, I would like an ice cream cone." The next question was, "Did he want one, two, or three scoops." He usually said, "Three scoops," and, "You kids get a cone for yourselves too." Then he gave us the money. Ice cream cones were five cents a scoop at that time. Hurrah! Another mission accomplished. The hard part was getting these big ice cream cones home without the ice cream falling off the cone. But they were so good!

When we were about eight, nine, and eleven, Daddy made a giant swing out of an old windmill. It was so tall that he had to get a big piece of machinery to pull it upright. We had so much fun on that swing. He put it on the large grassy part of the lawn fronting the creek, which he had made look like a park. He had planted weeping willow trees along the front edge of the river. It was just beautiful. To this day, I love weeping willow trees and have tried to grow one in Tucson. It didn't work as they needed much more water than we get in Tucson. To water them would cost too much of our precious water in the desert.

Our dad could build anything, and my youngest son is much like our dad. He became a welder like my dad. Unfortunately, he never knew my dad, as my dad passed away before he was born.

My dad applied for and received a couple of patents over the years. One was hauling gas in large drums for heating homes in the winter. A trailer with a drum held enough gas for several months for a home gas furnace. It was effortless for the gas companies to use and deliver the gas. Unfortunately, people could change one small thing that didn't infringe on the patent.

I have also tried to apply for patents, but others have had the same idea and received a patent. They haven't done anything with their patent. Usually, their plans are so extensive that implementing the idea wouldn't be cost-effective. It is disappointing when people apply for a patent, get it, and sit on it. If the patent is lifesaving, it is even more disappointing. My last idea is lifesaving, and I have tried several options with no success.

And now, going back to our childhood, we convinced the grocery store owner in Fisk that we needed a job. We assured him that giving us a job would help him. Can you not see him discussing this with children? How could we help him? We were so profound and trying to be convincing to an adult. It tickles me to this day. The owner and his wife were like an extra pair of grandparents.

They were friendly to everyone. The owner said we could help by picking out the spoiled potatoes from the larger bags of potatoes because "one spoiled potato spoiled the rest." We set to work finding those spoiled potatoes. I don't remember how long our "job" lasted, but we had fun, made a little money, and "helped" the owner.

We always enjoyed being at the store. We usually stopped on our way to school to pick up a snack. The school was so close that we always walked. They had all the fun kinds of penny candy sold at the time—even the candy cigarettes. That is the only kind of cigarette I ever smoked. I also liked all the peanut products sold at the time. I saved my money to buy the peanut head pen. It was a favorite of mine. We were so sad when the owners retired and sold the store.

Mom loved to watch movies, and when Daddy worked late at the shop, Mom would take us to a film in Omro. I remember the price was thirty-five cents, but I don't know if that was for Mom or kids. Whenever there was a coming attraction for a *Ma and Pa Kettle* comedy showing in the late 1940s, we just had to see it. Some of the movies were *At the Fair*, *On the Farm*, *At Home*, and *On Vacation*, to name a few. They were hilarious at the time. We couldn't wait for the next movie. We would watch the upcoming films and always had a couple we wanted to see. Of course, Mom always had some she wanted to see, so we had many choices each week.

We went to the theater about twice a week until Daddy bought a TV set in the late 1940s or early 1950s. Even though we weren't rich, we were one of the first families in Fisk to own a television. I guess Daddy thought it was safer than having his family drive to the movies twice a week. The neighbor kids would come over and watch with us. *Kukla, Fran, and Ollie* was one of the few shows at the time. It ran from 1947 to 1957, and all the kids loved it. I was not too fond of that program as it was too silly for me.

One time, we came home from the movies, and we all jumped out of the car. We ran to the house but didn't close the vehicle's doors. Mom didn't know it and drove the car into the garage. Daddy heard the noise at the shop across the street, and we all ran to see what had happened. To our dismay, the back two doors of the car, which opened to the back, were hanging. Yikes. We didn't know it, but Daddy had just sold the car the day before, and it was to be delivered the next day. He had to hurry and fix the doors. Our mom sat in the car with her head on the steering wheel. I don't remember being punished or not. But we did feel bad.

There was a window peeper in the neighborhood when we were kids. Mom kept telling Daddy she just felt someone was watching her, and one night, she called him at the shop across the street, and he came over to the house. He caught a man in the tree by our house and called the police. We lived a fascinating life as kids. Mom wasn't too excited, but she was happy that Daddy caught the guy. The neighbors knew who he was. That was the end of the window peeper!

There also was a house fire in the neighborhood. A house two lots over caught fire in the night, and the neighbors all went over to help. Being in the country, the fire station was far away, and by the time they came, the house was in bad shape. It was scary and exciting for us kids to look out the window and see the flames. Mom and Dad told us to "stay put" in no uncertain terms when they went to help.

The following day, we were allowed to go over and see the damage. It was devastating. The neighbor's dad had to shimmy down a tree in his birthday suit to get out of the house. It was a joke for a while, but he didn't think so. As I remember, the kitchen received the most damage. It took them time to rebuild the inside of the house and left quite an impression on the children. Fires took on a whole new meaning.

My dad liked to hunt, and he would go to Crivitz in Wisconsin to hunt deer around Thanksgiving time. Crivitz is about forty-five miles north of Green Bay, Wisconsin. Sometimes the whole family got to go along. The kids would sit on the bedding and boxes of stuff in the back seats while the adults sat in the front seats. It was so much fun. We couldn't wait to go again the next time.

We stayed in the cabins and played while the men hunted. We would caravan up, and that was also fun. The moms had supper ready when the men came back from hunting at the end of the day. The day's last meal is called supper in Wisconsin, not dinner as it is out west. We always had to be home for Thanksgiving supper at Grandma's house. There was no negotiation on that one with Grandma. All the hunters made their plans around that stipulation.

One time, we were eating in the car on the way up to Crivitz, and Mom gave me a banana to eat. I peeled it and threw what I thought was the peeling out the window. It was the banana! Remember, we were caravanning up to Crivitz, so the cars behind us saw this banana fly out the window at them. They never let me forget it. My brother teased me unmercifully for years afterward.

CHAPTER 3

Childhood Winters

The winter weather gave us several fun options as kids. If the water was high in the creek, it would freeze over thick, and we could go ice-skating. We patiently waited for it to freeze solid. It was always a big deal when the kids in the neighborhood could go ice-skating on the creek. For some unknown reason, I could ice-skate but not roller-skate. It doesn't make sense. At any rate, I loved to ice-skate with the other kids. And we did it as often as possible because the water didn't always get high enough to freeze so we could skate. Sometimes it didn't freeze over smoothly either.

Then there was sledding down the farmer's hill. We didn't use the road as it was too dangerous, but the large field next to the road was ours to use by the owners. And use it we did! Our paternal grandfather would pull our ten-people sled up the road in the winter with his car, and we kids and the neighbor kids would climb on and slide down the hill. Grandpa would pull the sled up the road again, and we would do it all over again. We did this until it became dark; we were either cold or tired.

My dad had made the large sled. It stayed in the family for years, and when we moved to Tucson for my dad's health, we gave it to my cousins. Thinking back and the precautions today, you can imagine what would be necessary to prevent an accident. We climbed on the sled, laid on each other three or four deep, and "hung on."

Because we were young and small, we could lay behind each other, so there were two rows, three or four deep! In today's world, we would need seat belts on everyone! Can't you see it?

My dad was an usher at church, taking that job very seriously. We went to church every Sunday. Mom put a "Sunday dinner" in the oven before we left so it would be ready to eat when we got home. Sunday dinner was a roast with potatoes, onions, and carrots. Our midday meal was dinner in the Midwest, and our evening meal was supper. When we got to Tucson, the midday meal was lunch, and the evening meal was dinner. That got us into trouble when we were invited to dinner, and we thought we were eating at noon and became very hungry by the time we ate at night.

We performed plays at Christmastime at the small school on a stage with curtains around the sides to hide the kids. I remember trying to be quiet, but we were all so excited that we kept laughing. The teacher would have to "shush" us.

The kids from all eight grades were in all the performances, so the little and older ones acted as moms and dads. It was so much fun for the kids. Moms made costumes for us, and we painted our faces to look young or old. We practiced for weeks to learn our parts. Those who knew how to play an instrument would play a song. I always wanted to play the accordion, and my friend knew how. She taught me one piece of music so that I could play it for my mom and dad. I was so proud.

We sang Christmas songs on planks set up like bleachers so that people could see all of us. One time when we were practicing, one of the kids fainted and fell off the plank. And with that, our practice was more exciting. The kid wasn't hurt—just totally embarrassed, as kids tend to be.

At the end of the program, Santa came and handed out gifts. Everyone got something. We always got a piece of fruit and pencils with our names from the teacher.

Our mom and dad always put up a real tree when Christmas came around. They would ask all of us kids what we wanted from Santa, and my first choice was always a doll. I usually got a new one every year. My sister liked dolls but didn't play with them much. So she usually didn't ask for a new doll each year. I always played with my dolls, and by the following year, I usually wanted a new one and was ready for another doll! My brother got trucks, but he asked for a doll one year—a boy doll. Wow! That didn't go over well in those days, and he didn't get a doll! A firefighter or police officer doll would have been an option, but it was just a no-no in those days. And there were no firefighters or police dolls anyway.

I love dolls and had over one hundred at once because of the company I worked for part-time. I have since given most of them away to my grandchildren, other children, and people I know who love dolls and the Gospel Rescue Mission in Tucson. The mission helps low-income families. I still have about thirty dolls.

While working for the company, one of the large dolls came with a broken leg. We always had to give damaged items to a charity, so we didn't have to pay for them or send them back to the company. The company allowed me to deal with a company that made artificial limbs for injured people. They made a leg that was removable from the doll and was authentic. They made it free of charge. We gave it to a little girl in Mexico who had lost the same leg.

The news media gave us the newsreel of the little girl getting the doll but wouldn't mention the company because they considered it an advertisement. I got a copy of the newsreel and sent it to the company. The little girl was so excited to get the doll.

We usually didn't get much for Christmas because Mom and Dad didn't have that much money, but we always got enough. The presents were never wrapped and were under the tree when they were delivered by Santa. In hindsight, there was no money for wrapping gifts. At any rate, that is what we expected, and we loved it. I tried it on my kids, who "weren't happy campers!" It didn't happen again.

One year, we all got used bikes for Christmas. Because of our financial situation, we were all older than you usually give a child a bike, but we were so excited that it just didn't matter. Our dad checked with all the farmers to see if they had any old bikes in their barn or garage, and he bought them and fixed them up for us. He found a girl's bike for my sister and a boy's bike for my brother but had difficulty finding a second girl's bike for me. He finally found one close to Christmas and had to hurry and fix it up. We found all the bikes under the tree—another successful Christmas.

Our dad built a dollhouse and a barn for us kids one year for Christmas. They were big! It had stanchions for the cows that worked, door handles, and all the little things you would find in a traditional barn. The dollhouse was typical, and I used to put wallpaper on the walls. I don't remember my sister playing with the dollhouse much, but she didn't enjoy dolls as much as I did, so it wasn't her "thing." When we moved to Tucson for my dad's health, Mom and Dad gave the barn and house to the one-room schoolhouse.

Years later, the school district sold the school. The new owners turned the school into a home. The teacher who taught us through the eighth grade and to whom my mom and dad gave the dollhouse and barn called me and said I could come to get them if I wanted them. I was so thankful for the opportunity to get them back that we immediately went over to get them. They were stored at the grand-parents' and later at my cousin's until we could have them sent to Tucson. I have them for our grandchildren.

My oldest son was so excited when he realized that I had them. He remembered playing in the barn where we had stored it at his grandparents' in Wisconsin. When I got divorced, we moved them to my cousin's basement. That was before I had them shipped to Tucson. I had forgotten that, and he remembered. It's good I moved them, or my ex probably would have burned them too. Later you will read how my ex burned our stuff in front of my oldest son.

When we couldn't play outside during the winter, our grandma Buehring came to visit more often. Our grandpa had passed away, and she would get lonesome, so she would get into her Studebaker and come from Oshkosh to Fisk for the day on Sundays. We could always hear the Studebaker come down the road, and we would run to the window to make sure it was Grandma coming. We loved to have her arrive as she always played cards with us.

She would stay for lunch and play canasta with us kids. She loved to play cards, and we kids loved to play with Grandma. If you remember canasta, you use more than one deck of cards. She would hold all the cards and click her false teeth while talking as if she didn't have anything in her hand. We saw she had many cards and thought she couldn't put them down all at once. Then she would surprise us, and all at once, she would put her whole hand down, and we would sit there with our mouths open in disbelief. Occasionally, we would be able to fool her and put our cards down first. She would say, "The nerve of some people's children," and we laughed. That was her favorite saying.

We kids could play cards well enough for the adults at the schoolhouse to let us play when they had card games. We had to pay for this honor just like the adults. We played and sometimes won. It wasn't a situation where the adults felt we weren't qualified. They liked us to play cards with them. It was fun, and everyone always had a good time. The card games were fundraisers for the school.

Sometimes my sister and I would play double solitaire. We used two decks of cards. We had our setup in front of each of us but played on only one set of aces through kings in the center, if you can imagine. The first one to see a place to put their card in the middle would do so. Sometimes we saw the opening at the same time and crunched the cards. My sister usually saw the spaces first and won. But occasionally, I beat her.

As we became old enough to drive, Daddy was the designated teacher, and he taught us. In addition to regular driving, we had to learn how to back into parking spaces, which was challenging for me. When Daddy felt we were ready, he took us to the sheriff for our test. The sheriff told Daddy that if he thought we could drive well enough, that was good enough for the sheriff. We never had to take the test. I was sixteen in 1957 when I got my license, and I drove from then on. (Until I got married!)

CHAPTER 4

High School

Because we lived in the country, we had to ride the school bus to Omro to attend the closest high school when high school came around. The other high school was in Oshkosh, but we were far away. That school was much more prominent. Having gone to a one-room schoolhouse, the smaller high school was better for us. Having fewer students, we could become friends with more people than in a large school.

Before high school, I had dieted earnestly because I didn't want to go to high school looking fat. The doctor had already found out why I was so chubby in grade school and put me on thyroid medicine by this time. I lost thirty-five pounds, was presentable, and could buy dresses off the shelf by the time I started attending high school. What a relief! It gave me such confidence—good, maybe bad. Sometimes my overconfidence got me into trouble. At this time in my life, my personality was different from when I got married. I was carefree and sure of myself. I was eager to try new things.

My sister was already a senior in high school when I was a freshman. The following year, my brother started high school. For some reason, the first-year girls in my class started dating the seniors. It was the first time so many first-year students had done that, and when that happened, the girls eventually started getting pregnant. Our class was the one with the most girls ever getting pregnant and, therefore, the smallest graduating class. It was not something we wanted to broadcast.

At the time, if you became pregnant, you couldn't continue school. It was exceedingly difficult on the girls because it cut their chances for better education and the opportunity to take care of their children. It is significant that people now understand that girls need education and are allowed to continue with it. So many girls in our class didn't finish high school. Most of the girls got married and raised their babies. They loved the baby's father, and the father was there for them. It was a different time!

During my high school years, we were encouraged to have pen pals. I chose one from Norway. We sent letters back and forth for several years. I wish that I had kept in contact with her. We learned much about each other's culture, likes, and land. I loved the books about Heidi and the fjords, so I chose to have a pen pal in Norway, where there are also fjords, and I loved Norway's scenery. Someday I would like to visit Norway.

We had home economics in high school then, and some of the boys even took the classes because they thought they would be easy. We learned how to make tapioca pudding, the only food I remember making, as I had never heard of tapioca pudding. It was delicious, and I still like it today. We also learned how to sew, something our mom often did. It was one of the best classes I could have taken because I made most of my clothes and those for our children from what I learned in class. I was proficient enough to design some of my outfits. After marriage, I taught my oldest daughter, who was in Blue Birds, how to sew. Their projects were at the county fair.

We had baseball and football games at the school, and some of us took the bus to towns outside Omro. They were mostly at night, and my friends and I loved to go. The athletic staff and cheerleaders were on a separate bus, and the students were on other buses. Mom and Dad usually said I could go. Once, it happened at the last minute, and I told my sister to tell Mom and Dad that I went to the game and friends would bring me home. She was not happy that I left it up to her to explain this piece of news to our parents. Of course, I didn't think anything of it.

We would sing about one hundred barrels of beer on the way up, and if we won, we would sing about them riding back. We were a noisy bunch! If we lost, we would usually sleep. One of my friends' parents would be at the school to take us all home. It was so much fun. Usually, my sister didn't go, and I didn't have to worry about staying with her. Our parents always believed we were safe because everyone said the bus driver was a "good guy." Later we discovered he was a pedophile. Now that was a troubling shock to everyone!

Yes, I, too, was dating a senior who had graduated by this time, and I was having a great time in school. I was the vice president of the sophomore class and was on the junior prom committee, which we decided to name "Honeycomb." The night of the dance, I ran to catch the hay wagon we were riding on and fell, scraping my knee terribly. My mom said she didn't think I should go to the prom! That didn't fly! I had a beautiful white ruffled dress, and there was no way I was staying home. So off we went, and we had a great time.

The senior boy was the only boy I had ever dated. I decided that I wanted to date others, so we broke up. I waited for someone to ask me out, but nobody did! Eventually, my senior boyfriend and I started dating again.

His sister was one of my best friends, and I told her that I couldn't understand why no one had asked me out. She told me *that my boyfriend, her brother, had threatened the boys that I was his girlfriend and they better not date me or have to answer to him.* ("Control and a first nudge of concern?") I will put in italics statements that people should look at as either control, physical, mental abuse, or concern. I want you to be sure to recognize the signs.

A week before moving to Tucson, my boyfriend asked me to marry him and gave me a diamond ring. He said he would move to Tucson to be with me. We were going to a basketball game that night, and I was so excited that I was standing in the bleachers, just flashing my ring for all the girls to see. And a week later, we moved.

My folks updated the kitchen to sell our home for the most money. Before we left Oshkosh, Mom had the kitchen of her dreams for a month or two. I always felt terrible that she couldn't have had the joy of that kitchen for much longer. She deserved to enjoy that kitchen. That was a good lesson for a young teenager. Don't upgrade something so others can enjoy it. Upgrade so you can enjoy it. That is what my husband and I are practicing as we grow older. We recently replaced the sliding glass doors in our primary bedroom with French doors. Expensive? Yes, but we enjoy them every day.

When we moved to Tucson, I was a junior in high school. My brother was a sophomore. My sister had already graduated, had a good job, and worked in Oshkosh. She wanted to stay in Oshkosh because she had a steady boyfriend. Our grandmother was getting on in years and offered to let my sister live with her. It was a good arrangement for everyone, and Mom and Dad didn't worry. My sister looked out for Grandma and had a nice place to stay, rent-free.

My mom and I cried the first whole day of the trip. The next day, Daddy said he "let us cry one day, and that was enough. Now we had to stop." My brother hadn't left anyone behind and was okay with the trip. Mom and I tried to get ourselves together for Daddy's sake. We knew we were going to Tucson for the chance at a better life for Daddy and fewer sinus infections and allergies. It still was hard for us!

The railroad stationmaster who worked in Fisk had moved to Tucson. Mom and Dad had become good friends with him and his wife. They offered to find us a place to rent before we got to Tucson. The idea was that we could just move in. Mom had seen homes in Tucson with carports, and she was picturing our rental as we drove into Tucson. She was so excited to see our place.

The rental market was terrible at that time. All the stationmaster could find was a rundown place. Mom thought the place was awful. It was dirty. The headboards had holes, and we envisioned what might be in the gaps. It was disgusting. Mom wouldn't eat there, so we ate all our meals in restaurants. Mom told Daddy to find us a home immediately. Daddy never let the grass grow under his feet and found a place to buy in a couple of days. We moved in about five days later. My mom lived there until she passed away at ninety-eight years old.

I had a good time at Omro High School and made many friends. They didn't offer any art classes in those days, and I loved art. I wish they would have had some art classes. The only thing I didn't like were the tests. I would study like crazy, and everything left my brain when I walked in the classroom door. Have you ever had the same problem? Also, one of the teachers used questions regarding items under the pictures on the test instead of important information. So if you studied the pictures, you would pass the test. The tests made no sense as to what we should be learning.

In Tucson, it was a different story altogether. The school was massive. We got to Tucson in March, so there were no lockers left for us, and we had to carry all our books to and from school. The administration said it was so close to the end of the school term that they would not try to find lockers.

My brother and I weren't used to getting to classes in such a big school. Because the classes were so far apart, we constantly ran between classes. I was always scared I wouldn't make it to my class in time and walk in late as a newbie. We were way behind in the course studies from Omro to Tucson, so we were always trying to catch up.

While getting to a class, once, I went out a door and found myself on the roof of the building. It locked behind me, and I couldn't get back in. It wasn't a fun experience. Finally, someone found me up there and let me back in. What a humiliation for the "newbie." I will *never* forget that day!

The weather was hotter in Tucson than in Fisk, and I would almost pass out whenever I was outside for a long time. We would get a ride to school in the morning but had to take the bus home in the evening. The bus had just passed on Speedway, where our bus stop was, when we got out of school, and we had to wait another thirty minutes for the next bus. Instead of staying in the heat, my brother and I usually walked home. If we walked, we would get home just when the bus would have come to our bus stop to pick us up on Speedway. We got home faster by walking. But it was so hot. Bless my brother's heart. He would take turns carrying my books because they were so heavy for me and I was so hot from the heat. He was a perfect brother.

After a while, my parents realized that our neighbors picked up their kids after school and agreed to pick us up when they got their kids. I would sit on the cement walkway at school to wait, and the heat would overcome me. I was close to passing out from the heat more than once.

In Omro, I was taking shorthand and doing very well; however, I couldn't understand the teacher when we got to Tucson. She dictated the letters for us to write down in shorthand. Because she had an accent, I couldn't understand what she said. How I passed that class is beyond me. While I couldn't understand what some people said to me, they wouldn't understand me either and would ask me to repeat something I said because they thought I had a funny accent from Oshkosh. We couldn't understand each other! They weren't poking fun at me. They thought my accent was cute. My brother and I both passed all our classes, thankfully. My brother went into the junior class, and I went into the senior class.

Four or five girlfriends took me under their wings and helped me navigate the school system. I will forever be grateful to them and wish I knew their names and addresses. They helped me with school, boy problems, and anything that came up. They were always there for me. If you read this book and recognize yourself, don't hesitate to get in touch with me. You can read me on Facebook in Tucson. I would love to hear from you. We went to the school the first year it was open. I believe it was Catalina High School on Pima Street. My class would have graduated in 1959. My brother was in the first graduating high school class, from first-year student through senior.

CHAPTER 5

Work in a Café and Marriage

Before senior year, I worked in a small café as a cook and server during the summer months. I was the only helper and worked with the husband and wife. One of the owners was a cook at Davis-Monthan Air Force Base and taught me some shortcuts to cooking. I still use them today. For example, don't peel the potatoes for a roast dinner. The peelings have nutrients in them. However, do wash the potatoes well.

To serve the breakfast crowd, the owners bought pie every day. One day, I mentioned that I could make the pies and save them some money. My mom gave me her recipe, and the next day, the cook said I should try and make some pies to see how they tasted.

The breakfast crowd was older adults, usually men, who went out for coffee and pie. They praised my efforts, so I started making pies every day. I don't know if they were good, but they gobbled them up. I guess anything was better than the ones purchased. It could also be that I was a cute young thing. Maybe? They did flirt with me.

During the summer months, my boyfriend called from Oshkosh and said he had been out on a date with someone else because I wasn't there, and he missed me. It hurt to think he would do that. *We were engaged to be married, and I believe we shouldn't be going out with others* (second *big* nudge of concern).

I was very hurt but forgave him, and he finally came out to Tucson. My dad had opened a filling station to have a job for him, and he lived with us to save my boyfriend's money. As there wasn't enough work for my dad and my boyfriend at the filling station, my dad got a job at Duval. My brother helped at the filling station when school was out.

I continued to work at the café, and we would go out to shows or wherever in the evenings. *One night, my boyfriend wanted more than just kissing. He had me on the car floor, and I kept saying, "Please don't, no, no!" But he wouldn't stop. He raped me. Everyone thought we were fooling around and had gone too far. No one set them straight, and that was that!* (Physical abuse—the third *big* nudge of concern!) It hurts to write this. My sister kept saying, "He raped you. I know he did." It took me over forty years to finally admit that he had raped me.

Life went on, and it became clear that I was pregnant, and I had to tell my mom. Like all the other girls in my class at Omro High School, I was pregnant! And with that, my school days were over. The schools in Tucson had the same policy as Omro. If you were pregnant, you could not go to school. My mom and dad were good about it and never asked questions. They helped me make plans for a wedding. My friends from school gave me a baby shower and helped me with everything. They made me feel "okay!"

Mom and I went to get shoes for the wedding, and they had a sale like they sometimes do at stores in Tucson where if you buy one pair, you will get another pair free. It made me happy and proud to save money by getting one pair for free. I showed my boyfriend my "deal." *He got mad that I had gotten two pairs of shoes. He said having two pairs of shoes was unnecessary and wouldn't accept that I hadn't paid for the second pair. He said it was frivolous of me to get two pairs of shoes.* (Control—the fourth nudge of concern!)

I had four nudges that should have concerned me before we married that there could be a problem. I should have taken all of them seriously. But I was too young, naïve, and trusting to realize it. If someone tries to control what you do or whom you see, that is a problem to be considered seriously in your relationship. With what you learn in this book, you should be more prepared than I was.

You may discover that male abusers usually have problems when male children are born into the family. Female abusers have issues when a female child is born into the family. I discovered this in our family. It may be just a coincidence, but I don't think so. I believe the abuser cannot accept the attention the significant other gives to the same-sex child of the abuser. They are jealous of their child. Our oldest was a male, and he was treated very differently than our girls. An abuser cannot accept the attention others put on their significant other. They become jealous and create an issue out of the situation. My family's affection was always a problem with my husband because he couldn't deal with their affection toward me.

My sister and grandmother came from Wisconsin, and we were married in August. I was seventeen. My parents made sure that I had a lovely wedding. I was married at our church, and we had the reception at home. The wedding was small because our family was in Wisconsin, and we hadn't made many friends yet in Tucson. But I was happy. My girlfriends from school were there to help me celebrate with the family. In all my pictures, I have a big smile. I was so happy to marry my high school sweetheart. It was raining as we left after the reception.

We went back to Wisconsin for our honeymoon, and I later realized the abuse had started on the honeymoon. We visited our families in Wisconsin, and his family and my sister had another reception. The family that couldn't come out to Tucson was at that reception. It was a much larger reception as most of our families lived in Wisconsin. My sister wanted our family side invited to the reception, so she agreed to help pay. She told me later that my husband's father thought everything was "too costly." My husband's family didn't want many things that my sister believed were necessary. Therefore, she agreed to pay for everything they questioned. My wedding cost her a lot of money and nerves.

After the honeymoon, my husband didn't want to go back to Tucson. But he had a job waiting for him, and my dad expected him to work it. *I had to pack everything myself because he wouldn't help* (control). We finally got on the road, but he got mad and took it out on me. He was upset as we drove back to Tucson.

We had rented a small one-bedroom home and moved in. I knew nothing about cooking, which was fun, but I am a quick learner and made out okay with my mom's help. Even though we had some cooking classes in high school, I didn't do any cooking at home as my sister did all of it while my mom was at work. So when I got married, it was a disaster. Gravy? What is that? You never saw so many lumps in all your life. With practice comes perfection, and over time, I became an excellent cook and loved to bake—bread, pies, cookies, donuts, and even homemade jam. The freezer was always full of baked goods. Did you know that if you made bread on a rainy day, the bread turned out much softer? When it rained, I always tried to bake bread. Also, put a bit of mashed potato in the bread, which will make the bread softer and taste better. The kids got tired of homemade bread, if you can believe it!

I was still working at the café, so I made a little money. At the time, I believe my husband let me keep the money I made to buy baby clothes and go to the doctor. I just loved getting the baby clothes. In those days, we didn't know the sex of the baby and couldn't get pink or blue. I would buy "one-piece sets," diapers, baby shirts, and anything for a baby. I wanted a new baby bed, and my husband said a used one was good enough. Of course, I wanted a new one for our baby. With the family's help, we got a new one.

My dad took my husband to the bank and introduced him to the banker who set up a combined bank account. The banker also changed all my information to reflect my new name. My time in Tucson was the only time in my married life with my husband that I had a combined bank account. The bank account was in his name only for thirteen years when we lived in Wisconsin.

Life went on. My husband continued to work at the filling station for my dad. He was the person to open the station as my dad was working at the Duval mine. But my husband did not take the job seriously and would not get up to get to work on time. I would set the clock early so he wouldn't know it and hopefully got to work on time. That didn't work. It was a persistent problem. It was very unpleasant because he worked for my dad, and I felt responsible. My dad never said anything to me, but I knew it was a problem because my dad was a conscientious worker.

I went into labor, and my husband took me to the hospital. *He waited until after our son was born, and then he called my parents to tell them the baby was born. He teased Mom on the telephone about not telling her where I was—what hospital.* (Mental abuse?) My husband thought he was funny. My mom became upset, and my dad asked her for the phone. In no uncertain terms, Dad asked where I was. There was no further discussion. Such instances created problems between my parents and us. My husband didn't want to be in Tucson, so he didn't care what he said or if it caused a problem.

When my dad bought a product for the filling station, he would eventually get coupons and a gift. One of the gifts my brother wanted, and my dad said he could have it. When it came in, my husband took it.

I was unaware that my husband was calling and writing to Oshkosh to get a job, and he finally got one. He then told me that he had an appointment and we had to be in Oshkosh in a given number of days. To keep the family together, I had to pack and go along. That left my dad with a filling station with no worker and days to find a replacement. We rented from a friend, leaving him with a house and no renter. *None of that was a problem for my husband. He had what he wanted, and that is all that mattered.* We were on the road in a few days, and everyone was left holding the bag. Our baby boy was only a few months old. My mom was devastated to see us go.

When we left, my husband took all the money out of our bank account in Tucson and closed it. When we got to Oshkosh, *he only opened a new bank account in his name. When I proved myself, he told me my name would go on the account. What does that mean? I didn't know what I had to do to prove myself. I don't think my name ever went on the account* (control). He wouldn't tell me what I had to do to prove myself. Finally, I quit asking for my name to be on the account! It was humiliating that I was not on the bank account as an adult.

We stayed at his parents' home when we went back to Wisconsin. They had a large farmhouse, two-story, with many bedrooms. We had a room that was downstairs, open, and had no door. You had to walk past our room to get from one end of the house to the other, and it was one way to get to the upstairs bedrooms. We were in a fishbowl.

It had been several weeks, and I told my husband we needed to find a place for the family. But he was satisfied with the situation as it was. I heard of a home for rent down the road and went to talk with the owners. The rent was very reasonable, and I convinced my husband we should move. We still ate with his parents every Sunday. The Sunday meals went on for several months and were getting tiresome. After some discussion, we ended the weekly meals with his parents.

CHAPTER 6

Moved Out of In-laws

While we were still living at my in-law's house, my mother-in-law started to make appointments for me. She believed I was too young to realize the baby needed his shots and made doctor appointments. She told me when the dates were—like within the week. It was a shock that someone would make such appointments and expect me to follow through on them, especially when I was not allowed to drive.

I complained to my husband. His mother just presumed I would use their doctor. I had my doctor that I wanted to see. After telling my mother-in-law that I was capable of making the appointments, I made the appointments but had to use their doctor. I had to have someone from the family take the baby and me to the appointment, *which was with their doctor.* (Control.)

His mother also was making arrangements for the baby to be baptized. By this time, I was getting upset because they thought I was not competent enough to take care of the baby. His mother said they should make the arrangements if they paid the costs. These assumptions were getting to me. I told her we would pay for the food and make arrangements. And I did. They finally realized that I could take care of my child at eighteen. Those issues never came up again, and I believe they had more respect for me.

When a man married a woman in his family, the woman became his property. You no longer had any rights because you were a possession. It was a very outdated take on life, but it was my reality. My family had never lived like that, and I was unaware that any family lived that type of life. It was a hard lesson that I no longer controlled my own life. Someone else was telling me what I could do.

We had moved out of his parents' home and now lived down the road. Because my name was not on the bank account, I had to walk over a mile down to his parents' home if I needed to buy something, usually a gift for my husband. I had to carry the baby as I wasn't allowed to drive. I would give his dad the cash, and his dad would write a check from his bank account for the order I wanted. His dad would mail the statement, and I would wait for the order to be received.

My money was now controlled totally by my husband and his father (control). Previously, I had an account in my name from when I started making money as a youngster until I got married and moved back to Oshkosh. But my husband said I couldn't use money wisely. How he came up with that piece of knowledge, I do not know; however, it was true because he said so. I am not aware that my name was ever on our bank account. I asked several times, and he gave the same answer—*when I proved myself, my name would go on the account* (control). I was so humiliated that I just gave up asking.

As proof that I could not handle money, he would give me about twenty dollars when I needed makeup, feminine products, or the children needed something (control). He pointed out that I spent all of it immediately, which was true. By the time he gave me any money, the children and I needed so many things that the twenty dollars could have been fifty, and it still wouldn't have been enough. He would let me order school clothes through a catalog, and he wrote the check.

Our son was my pride and joy because he kept me centered when my husband was abusive. One day, I just rocked him in the rocker, holding him tight, and said to him, "What have I done to us?" He was such a good baby, and I was so miserable. It was less than six months after his birth and into our marriage. He wasn't allowed to cry because it bothered my husband. If I didn't stop his crying immediately, *my husband would go into the bedroom and spank him until the bed shook* (physical abuse). Now both of us would be crying. *My husband pushed me out of bed if I was in bed when he started crying and I didn't get up quickly enough* (control).

As my son grew, he learned to crawl over the crib's railing and down the side to "escape." He thought that was so funny. Of course, as a mother, it scared me to think he could fall. He never did.

I tried to nurse the babies but was so nervous that my body would not cooperate and "let the milk down." It made me feel like another failure. *My husband said that if I were a cow, they would have gotten rid of me long ago because I didn't make money* (mental abuse). When a woman married into this family, she didn't have any rights. It was sad but true to realize it too late.

In the late 1950s and early 1960s, you could purchase plastic curtains for the windows. That was all I could afford for our house, and I bought them at the Woolworths department store in Oshkosh. As a newlywed, I was so excited about those curtains. Little things excited me in those days.

For the thirteen years we were married, I always worked at Christmas to have money for my family's gifts and sometimes even for the kids. Nothing was equal in our marriage. *If he wanted something, there was no discussion—he bought it: a snowmobile, a brand-new truck every two years, a trip to Canada with the guys, no problem. It had to be necessary and low maintenance if I wanted something like a dishwasher. Nothing fancy because that product costs too much money and breaks down* (control). The only time I got something nice was when he had just beaten me up and was trying to make up, and then I would get a vacuum or something like that. *I got a dishwasher once but promised not to use the dry cycle to save money* (control). After the divorce, I didn't know how to use the drying cycle when I bought a dishwasher.

I started using the new birth control pills just approved for pregnancy control when I was nineteen. My husband had no part in birth control. The birth control pills seemed to cause migraine headaches and blood clots in my legs, but the doctor didn't seem concerned. But it did concern me because of my legs' extensive bruises. I decided to stop the pills and see what would happen. The bruises stopped but not the migraines. The migraines never did stop, and I later learned that the hormones in the birth control pills did cause the start of the migraines. Doctors finally agreed that was the cause because so many women developed migraines after taking the birth control pills. I told my daughters not to take the pills. I am eighty-one and still get migraines, but they are not as severe.

Migraines are excruciating headaches. The pain is so bad that you start vomiting, get diarrhea, and need intervention by a doctor. The headache will last for at least three days if you can't see a doctor. Some people require hospitalization and strong pain medication. Hormones, stress, allergies, and even a change in atmospheric pressure can bring them on. Red wine and onions also bring them on for me. Usually, you don't get them as often as you get older.

By this time, my parents knew what was going on in our marriage. They would send me things for Christmas that they knew I needed but couldn't purchase, like underwear. That is the only time I would have nice lingerie, and I could count on getting them at Christmas. That is the only thing I remember getting from my parents—underwear. I know they gave me many other beautiful things, but the underwear is what made the biggest impression.

Before my husband would go to work, *he would make me write out a list of the things I promised to accomplish that day because he was afraid I would sit and watch soap operas all day long. When he got home from work, I had to show him what I had all crossed off the list* (control). Can you call that forced labor?

We went to counseling twice—once with a counselor and once with the pastor. When we went to the counselor, my husband would not tell the truth about what was happening and denied anything I said. We would leave and fight all the way home. When he heard about the money situation, the pastor sat us down and told me, "Sandra, how much money do you think you would like for a month?" Never having *any* money before, I said something ridiculous like twenty dollars. We settled on a minor amount of money. The physical abuse was downplayed by my husband and eventually returned. But the pastor did help me for a while.

As the kids grew, it became hard for me to show my love for them because of my husband's hurtful words. I felt I couldn't trust people who said they loved me. I knew the kids loved me, but would they turn on me too? I had to teach myself to show the kids my affection by sitting on the sofa with them and deliberately hugging them. I told them how much I loved them. How sad that you must learn to trust people because of how others treat you. Now we hug each other whenever we meet, and I am a hugger. I tell people when I meet them that I am a hugger and warn them should they not want a hug. Usually, they smile and hug me first.

CHAPTER 7

Carol's Wedding

My sister called one day and said they had set a date for their wedding. The first thing out of my mouth was, "Oh no, I'm pregnant."

She asked, "How far along?"

And I said a day or two. She said not to worry and that I was just late. Notice, I was *never* late. If I was a day overdue, I was pregnant. And yes, it turned out I was pregnant.

I stood up for my sister at about seven or eight months pregnant. I was the matron of honor, and one of my sister's fiancé's brothers stood up as the best man. My husband was also a part of the wedding party. Of course, the brother didn't want to stick around with a pregnant woman, *and my husband thought it was his place to stay with his partner at the wedding.* (I don't know what this is—just that it was abusive to me.) I was alone during the wedding, and my husband was the life of the party.

Whenever someone said they were getting married and asked me to be a part of the wedding, I was pregnant. It got to be a joke after a while. We finally broke the cycle when my sister-in-law, whom I loved like a sister, called to say she was getting married and wanted me to stand up for her at the wedding. There were shouts of joy all around. I could stand up in a regular dress! It was fun to feel normal at a wedding, dance finally, and enjoy myself. I remember that I wore a beautiful lilac dress. It was a fitted dress and showed my curves!

Speaking about being pregnant, it seemed my friend and I would get pregnant about the same time. We both had four children of about the same age. One time, my friend called. She told me how sick she was, how she felt so big, and all the other things pregnant women tell each other. I was also pregnant but hadn't told her, so I sympathized with her. She would call a few days later and tell me how miserable she was. Finally, she realized I was in the same boat. I got a big kick out of fooling her. We were good friends, and our kids got along well together. My husband and I and she and her husband went out dancing almost every week.

The kids dentist was a wonder with kids. He said that we needed to pull one of the teeth on each side of the top and bottom of our two oldest children when they were young. He explained that if we did, they wouldn't need braces. They didn't. One innovative dentist saved his patient's parents much money by not paying for braces if they listened to him. I had a time getting my husband to agree to pull "good teeth" from the two kids' mouths, but they have beautiful teeth today. I didn't remember that and probably couldn't have afforded it when the two youngest children were my responsibility in Tucson.

Living on the farm, we had lots of flies in the house in the summer. The usual way to get rid of them was with the ugly, sticky hanging strips. I read in a newspaper that if you put powdered dish soap in a cup with water and put that on a long rod, you could walk around the room at night when they were sleeping on the ceiling. The soap would make the fly's legs give way, and they would fall into the glass and drown. So I tried it—and it worked. That was my job before bed at night—to get the flies off the ceiling. It was an easy way to catch the flies, and there were no ugly fly strips. Just remember that you have to use powdered dish soap. Who would think it could be so easy?

I had stress-related illnesses while married. Because of the stress from the abuse, sometimes, I would be in a crowded situation and go completely blind. Doctors called it blind hysteria. It lasted until people moved away from me and gave me room and air, and then I could see again. It was terrifying. I hung on to the person beside me so I wouldn't fall. It would happen in a crowd, at a dance, and even in church. Sometimes it would be so bad that I would start getting sick. It gradually disappeared after I divorced and moved to Tucson with the kids. Stress can be hard on the body and show up in many ways.

Taking control of a situation for the abused isn't something to do with a person you know is in an abusive relationship. The following is an excellent example of what can happen. We went with the rest of the family to my cousins' for dinner. The three kids were with us. I hadn't had the last son yet. After dinner, my husband was ready to leave. It was embarrassing to eat and go, and my cousin noticed me talking with my husband. She pulled me aside and asked what was happening, and I said he wanted to leave. She said, "You come with me. We'll go in the other room, and he will forget about it." My husband didn't say anything. He knew how to control himself and was nice when we were out. No one realized what he was really like at home. Everyone thought he was terrific. They were unaware of how I was treated at home when no one was around but him and me. My daughter says they noticed but didn't want to get involved.

When we finally left, he yelled as we drove home and after we got home. The kids were crying in the back seat. All my going into the other room did was infuriate him further, and it was worse for me. So take this as a lesson for those that want to help—don't step in like this. I don't think anything would have been a solution except to let us leave and say something like, "We hope you can stay longer next time."

People who want to help the abused need to understand that if the abuser believes you are trying to interfere, they will make sure *you* are out of that person's life. They will not let you talk to them on the telephone or meet for coffee or anything. You must do it without them knowing it.

The abused must have a place to be safe if they are leaving. Only by moving two thousand miles away was I safe. And I was going where my family was. Only *his* family, close relatives, and friends were in Wisconsin, and I had no support system. His family knew how the family operated and would not interfere. Our friends did not know.

Somehow, you need to establish a support system for the person. Be *sure* the support system is on the abused side, not the abuser. And *never* leave your kids. You want your kids to have a safe life also. They need to get away from the abuse as well as you do. If I ever had suicidal thoughts, I immediately got rid of them. There was no way I would let my husband or his family raise our children.

If you ever have suicidal thoughts or believe you have mental issues that need to be addressed, get help *immediately*! This is not something you should be ashamed of, as we all have problems sometimes. Your kids need you, and you need to realize that your life is worth everything. I have known people who committed suicide, and their families suffered greatly. You do not want to bring that into your family. The *National Suicide Prevention Lifeline is 1-800-273-8255*. They are open twenty-four seven for help. You can also call 988, a new three-digit number that became available on July 16, 2022.

When Christmas came around, my husband bought gifts for his family—a refrigerator for his mom and whatever he thought his dad wanted. We didn't have money for my mom and dad, which hurt me (control).

I started working around Christmas at a small restaurant to get gifts for my family. They had homemade Italian foods, and I could have some money to buy my family Christmas presents. I had only worked at the café in Tucson as a teenager and was the only server there. I didn't know how to enter and exit the kitchen—the right door to enter and exit the kitchen. <u>If you always go to the right, you will be okay!</u> All the salads hit the floor the first time through the wrong door. The other servers quickly showed me the ropes. I also started working at the restaurant to help myself become more outgoing. Due to the abuse, I was introverted. As a teenager, I was happy and outgoing. By getting the job, I hoped interacting with the customers would make me more outgoing. And it did.

It was fun working at the restaurant, especially with the children. I always carried crackers in my pockets to have something to tide them over if they got hungry and the food wasn't ready. The parents appreciated that.

All the staff could get two free drinks a night. The cook liked to drink, and she knew she could ask me to go to the bar and ask for a drink with my other drink order, and they wouldn't question me—at first. The bartender knew what her drink of choice was. After a while, they caught on and said they wouldn't fill her order anymore that night. I couldn't lie; if the bartender asked if it was for the cook, he could tell just by looking at my face. By that time, she had had at least four drinks! She was a happy cook!

Our boss became ill, and when he passed away, all of the workers met at the restaurant before going to the memorial. We all had a couple of drinks. I liked a drink that tasted like lemonade, so I thought the bartender wasn't putting much liquor in until I almost fell off the chair. It didn't take much to get me tipsy!

One Christmas, my oldest son got to the age where he thought he "knew" there was no Santa Claus and was quite sure of himself. He knew he was a big boy and should no longer believe in Santa Claus. He was about six, and we had his younger sister, who was four and a half. I told him not to let on to his little sister.

Even with the abuse, I could do things to make the kids excited. So I thought, *I will have fun with him.* I arranged with our neighbors, my great friends, that she and her husband would come over and put the toys under the tree, drink the wine left for Santa, and eat the cookies while we were gone. I have no idea why I chose to put out wine instead of hot chocolate.

When we came home, we deliberately let our son go in first. He thought he would prove there was no Santa and happily went in first. He was stunned when he saw all the toys under the tree. He knew we had walked in after the kids and couldn't understand how all the toys got there. He never did ask me.

The next day, the neighbor called me to see how it went. She said her husband got sick and she had to come alone. The two houses were about one-half of a block from door to door, and there were two glasses of wine and double cookies. She was teasing that she had difficulty drinking the two glasses of wine and was still able to walk home. I guess she didn't think to pour one down the drain. Anyway, it was fun playing the joke on our son.

When the kids were little, about six and seven, a new church was starting down the road. The two oldest kids were very good at singing and joined the children's choir. The mothers made capes as choir robes with big red bows for the fronts. We couldn't figure out how to get the large bows to stay put. We finally got as many men's bow ties as we could and used the clips to sew them onto the red bows, which worked perfectly. Being able to sew, I helped make as many as possible. The kids looked adorable, and they all sang so sweet. They sang for several years until my oldest son's voice changed.

In one house we rented, an upstairs bedroom was set up as the sewing room, with the sewing machine always open and the ironing board up and ready. Because I never had money to get the kids many clothes for school, I would make their clothes. I was a pretty good seamstress and even designed some of my clothes. I could run upstairs and sew on their clothes if there were a few extra minutes. I made the girls' sunsuits when they were tiny and fancy ruffled panties. They always were dressed cutely because I could make the clothes cheaply.

For my oldest son, I made him regular shirts like men wear, and they aren't that easy to sew in the sleeves if anyone has stitched shirts. He had quite a few ready when he went to first grade. He looked like a regular little man, and I was proud of him. He came home from school one day and said, "Mom, can I have shirts like the other kids?" The other kids had T-shirts and were making fun of his shirts. Sometimes, moms try too hard to be good moms.

I don't remember what I said, but I sure hope I said, "Yes," and got him T-shirts. My son said I did; every year after that, he got regular T-shirts for school. I was such a protective mom. It wasn't fathomable that I wouldn't "save him" from the kid's teasing.

One week, I took the kids to a park to ride the ponies. We had three kids at the time, and they all got on a pony. My youngest daughter started screaming because she was afraid, and I told the trainer to get her off the pony. He didn't comply because he didn't want to stop the other kids' fun. This mommy ran into the arena and stopped the ponies. He immediately took my daughter off the pony, and the rest continued their ride! The other moms clapped. My daughter stopped crying in "Mommy's arms."

It seemed that *whenever we went someplace, my husband got agitated* (mental abuse). The kids were all lined up in the back seat in their cute little clothes and happy. On the way home, he would find something to get upset about, and we would get home with all the kids crying in the back seat. It was so disheartening that we couldn't enjoy a good time out.

If I wanted to go and see my family in Tucson, my husband wouldn't pay for the trip. *I had to get a job and save all of my checks. When we left to go to Tucson, I had to cash all the paychecks at once. He expected all the money. Before we left, he sat in the car and counted the money he had in his wallet. He then ensured that he had that much in his wallet when we returned. I had nothing in my purse. We went to Tucson twice in the thirteen years, with me paying for everything* (control).

When we got to Tucson, my husband was so jealous that *I had to "take care of him" before I could go and spend time talking with my mom and dad* (control). He would bug me until my mom would say, "Go and take care of him and then come out and talk with us." It was very embarrassing.

The first time we went to Tucson, my oldest son was just about three, and he was outside my parents' home playing. The following day at breakfast, his little face grimaced when he sat down. My mom saw it and asked him what the matter was. He tried to explain about the cactus out front and how he fell on it with his little behind. Mom pulled my little son's pants down, and his bottom had cactus pricks everywhere. My dad was a very quiet man. He wasn't able to show his feelings well. But when he saw my son's discomfort, he felt the pain too. My dad got up from the table and removed the cactus. Daddy always had his priorities straight!

When my class was to graduate from high school in Omro, my husband, baby, and I were in the garden planting potatoes. It wasn't a good night for me as I was very depressed. The cars of my classmates would go by and beep their horns at us. They were all so excited and happy. They didn't realize I was sad because I wouldn't be graduating with them. I was sad that I wasn't graduating as I was smart and should have been. My siblings had all graduated, my sister was valedictorian, and my brother had even graduated from college. I promised myself that I would graduate from high school and walk up to get my diploma.

CHAPTER 8

Graduation from High School

That promise that I would graduate high school played on my mind. To fulfill that promise I made to myself, I went to the high school in Omro where I should have graduated to discuss with the guidance counselor whether they would let me return to school and complete the classes I needed. If a girl was pregnant, she couldn't continue school, and I had been pregnant in my senior year in Tucson and couldn't continue. The counselor told me they had enough trouble with the kids currently in school and didn't have time for people like me. It was like a kick in the stomach. This counselor had been one of my favorite teachers at Omro High School, and I was devastated by his attitude.

Not to be discouraged, I called Mom and Dad and asked if they would pay for the first class I needed through the University of Wisconsin. I told them that I would pay for the rest. I needed three classes to graduate. It didn't sound like much, but it took a long time. They were pleased that I wanted that diploma so seriously and happily agreed. That's when I started on my journey to earn my high school degree—two years after I should have graduated. I was nineteen years old.

In high school, they were taking plane geometry, while in the college class I had to take, they were teaching spherical geometry. Spherical geometry was so much more difficult. It took longer than usual to get through each class because I had to write to the professor to ask a question, and he responded, "You tell me!" Now that wasn't very helpful. On top of that, I couldn't picture the problem of spherical geometry in my mind. In desperation, I got out my son's tinker toys and built the problem, and then I could "see" it. It worked like a charm. Sometimes you think "way outside the box!"

It took a while to get money for the next class each time because I had no access to cash. And I took the final course through the school so that I could march up with the group and get my diploma in person. That was very important to me—I wanted to walk across that stage. They let me do that. It took several years for me to get all the classes in. Finally, I did it.

When the time came to graduate, I had my cap and gown, and all three of my children at the time were in the audience to see me graduate. I was about twenty-five at the time. *My husband couldn't understand the significance of wanting pictures of me in a cap and gown and getting my diploma. To him, it was no big deal. But to me, it was a huge deal. He didn't want to take the camera, and I only had pictures taken at the house.* (Mental abuse? Control? You decide.) My mother-in-law had a party with cake to celebrate my graduation. It meant a lot to me.

That was a real lesson for our kids on how important a high school diploma was. The three oldest remember sitting there, watching me go across the stage, and hearing my name called. My diploma reads Sandra Buehring O'Neill to honor my parents.

Eventually, after the divorce and living in Tucson, I earned enough college credits for one and a half years. I hoped to get a college degree, but it took so long because I was working more than one job at a time for income. It took time away from the kids and earning a living, so I decided to stop and enjoy our lives of freedom. It was worth it. The classes I did take helped me advance in the workplace. I worked my way up to second-in-command in our division.

One Christmas, while still married, we drove out to Tucson. My husband built a camper for the truck. We only had two children, and I was pregnant with the third. My doctor said it was okay to make the trip. However, I don't think he realized I had to scrunch through the back window to get into the camper while my husband was driving. One night, it was late, and my husband was tired and almost went off the road. I tend to fall asleep as soon as I get in a car, which doesn't help to keep him awake. I told him to go into the camper with the kids to get some sleep. I slept on the front seat of the truck.

All at once, someone was trying to wake me up. I could smell something but tried to go back to sleep, but again someone tried to wake me up. I finally came fully awake, and the camper was full of smoke. I started yelling for my husband to wake up, and he kicked out the camper's back door. A blanket had fallen over the heater and began to smoke. I am pretty religious and believe my "someone" was a guardian angel who woke me. It wasn't our time yet. Others might have different beliefs, but that is what my faith will always be. Please don't be turned off by my religious beliefs. We all have our views. Just insert whatever your belief is in place of mine. You will see little notes like this throughout the book. My beliefs are an integral part of my life.

Because my dad passed away so young, I asked my oldest son if he remembered his grandpa, and he said he sure did. He told me his grandpa would eat his egg yolks because he didn't like them. I am sure my son got into trouble with his father for not eating them, which is why he remembers this meaningful gesture by his grandpa.

When my dad was dying of cancer at fifty-four, I wanted to see him one last time. My cousins were making a trip to Tucson and agreed to take our youngest daughter and me along so it wouldn't cost me as much. *My husband didn't think the trip was necessary. I don't know if he gave me the money—probably not—or I worked for it, or my mom gave it to me, but I had about $500 for my daughter and me both ways* (control). My daughter wasn't in school yet, and I didn't think her father could care for her. The older two kids were in school. I left them at home, hoping they would be okay while I was gone.

I was hoping I would only have to share the gas, pay for our lodging, and eat. My cousins asked if I would pay for the accommodations instead of gas. My cousin insisted on staying at expensive places. It turned out that this was more expensive than the gas would have been and cost me more than was expected. We were almost home when I ran out of money. I offered to pay for their meal and worked to repay them when we got home. My mom didn't know this until several years before she passed. She was upset with me for not asking for money before leaving Tucson. It is tough for me to ask for help.

My daughter got car sick, and we had to stop several times. When we got to Tucson, my daughter was so excited to see her grandpa that she ran up to him in the hospital, grabbed him around the legs, and almost knocked him over because he was weak. She was about five years old at the time. My dad wanted me to think he wasn't so bad, so he insisted on coming home from the hospital while we were there. He came and ate at the table and talked with us, acting as if he was in great shape. My mom said she had to take him back to the hospital as soon as we left.

We weren't home very long when my dad passed away, and I wanted to go back for the funeral. *Again, my husband said I had just been there and seen my dad and didn't need to return* (control). My mom came through and paid for me to fly back. Other cousins met me in Chicago and flew with me to Tucson. I was very young—twenty-eight at the time—and had never flown before. None of the kids went with me that time.

If I did something my husband didn't want me to do, he would *yell at me, grab me by my arms, and pinch me so hard that there would be marks on my arms showing all his fingerprints* (physical abuse). Once I managed to hold him back and scratch him. His mother saw the scratch marks and asked what had scratched him. My husband said a cat, and she said she would get rid of the cat if it were her! I didn't say anything.

One time, I went to my uncle's funeral with a black eye (physical abuse). It was very embarrassing to attend a funeral with bruises on your face. All of my family members wanted to know what had happened. *Once, he punched me in the stomach when I was pregnant* (physical abuse). They say it is a significant sign of an abuser hitting a pregnant woman in the stomach. Why? I don't know if they are already jealous of the child, but it happened to me. *He yelled at me about how "stupid" I was or that I couldn't do something because I was too "dumb."* If they want *to determine where you are, whom you are with or talking to, what names are on your cell phone, how long you will be gone, and what you are buying,* which are forms of controlling you, these are the top abuse issues. *Heed the warning!* These are examples of being abused. And *you* didn't deserve it, as they will claim. *You* didn't do anything to provoke them. No, it is *their* responsibility to "own" the action.

Money was a way he controlled me. I had none (control). He drove to the store and sat in the car with the kids when we went shopping. He gave me twenty dollars for the groceries and anything else I might need for the week. The twenty dollars had to last the whole week. If I ran out, I didn't get any more. Twenty dollars was also supposed to cover my clothes, gifts, and everything else. Once, groceries cost almost the entire twenty dollars at the store. I had nothing left to pay for the bread delivery during the week or anything else we might need. Too bad! I didn't get any more money because I was irresponsible and should have kept track of how much the groceries cost.

If I wanted to do something, he would say, "What makes you think *you* can do that (mental abuse)?"

You have probably noticed the change in tone during this portion of the book. While the first part was bubbly and happy, this part is only factual. I cannot seem to find laughter and fun during this time of my life.

We will have to get through this portion of our lives knowing good times are ahead. Keep with me.

Time went on, and the physical and mental abuse gradually got worse. I took out divorce papers twice during this time, and my husband convinced me each time that he would never hit me again. All that happened was that I had two beautiful girls and another sweet little boy. *Before we went to the hospital, he insisted that he get fed. I had to make him lunch or supper, and then we would go to the hospital.*

When I got home, the dishes would still be in the sink. His excuse was that "men" didn't do dishes. I would never give up my children, but living like that was hell for the kids and me. They went wherever I went. I don't think my ex enjoyed this life either, but he didn't change.

My husband always had me cut his hair to save money. *He waited until the day we were going out, and I had to cut his hair before getting myself ready. Sometimes he would wait until the last minute to say he needed his hair cut, making me rush around to get myself ready. Everything was on his timetable and made me a nervous wreck* (mental abuse). I could watch him walk from the barn to the house when he got home from work and "know" if I would "get abused" that night. You could tell by his walk! I am sure some of you reading this understand.

I loved to cook, and one night, I made steak, baked potatoes, sweet corn, and fancy gelatin in glasses for supper. We had three children at the time, and we all sat down at the table to eat. I was so excited about the meal I had prepared. The gelatin didn't stick to the sides of the glasses, *so my husband just slipped his out and made believe it was his breast. He just laughed and laughed and thought it was so funny* (mental abuse). It wasn't amusing to me, and I "snapped." I threw a steak knife at him, which thankfully missed, and ran into the bedroom sobbing.

I genuinely believe I would have had a nervous breakdown if I hadn't broken down. That is certainly not something you want your kids to see. The knife broke the glass windows, and we had to replace them. It was an awful night for the kids and me. My husband said nothing.

I cry very quickly at frustrations, and I believe it is a coping technique from that time in my life.

My oldest son recently said, "Not everything is abuse, Mom. Some of it is just plain mean-spirited." So when you read this book, it will be up to you to decide if it is control, abuse, "just plain mean-ness, or harassment" by the person. I will leave it up to you. At any rate, *you* don't need to continue living with it. If you think it is not abuse, as you read the examples of control, mental abuse, and physical abuse, maybe you are going through the same thing but do not want to recognize it as abuse. Think about that!

Finally, we had a lull in the abuse. My mind was always working overtime, and I wrote a letter to the Oshkosh Newspaper People's Forum. We had an outdoor theater called the 44 Outdoor Theater. It had a giant screen and a play area for the children before the show began. However, there were hardly any shows that a parent could take their children to that were "family-friendly." I sent a letter asking the theater management to set aside one night weekly for "family night." They agreed, and we had movies to take the kids to for a while.

While management showed family-friendly movies, families didn't participate, and the administration stopped the family nights. How sad. I had tried, but the people didn't follow through on a good thing. I was thoroughly disappointed with the families.

For one summer, I worked at the University of Wisconsin Oshkosh Campus. I worked for two professors teaching a master's program. The program gave the students a master's degree for studying over the summer months. The purpose of the class was to show that people thought ahead about "what they would say" instead of listening to "what people were saying" at the time. It was an exciting and thought-provoking class. One of the professors moved to Tucson eventually as his family was from Tucson.

While working at the university, I became pregnant with my fourth child but wasn't aware of it until I was five months pregnant. I was trying to lose weight and just couldn't. My neighbor and I had joined TOPS, taking off pounds sensibly. I finally went to the doctor to see if I was sick. Nothing led me to believe anything was wrong, and I couldn't understand why I couldn't lose weight. He said I was five months pregnant. What? I was still having my monthly periods!

Before I became pregnant for the fourth time, friends had done the "what will the baby's sex be" on my wrist before the third baby was born. They hung a needle on a string and held it over my wrist. The needle twists in one direction for a boy and the other direction for a girl. It registered one boy and two girls, waited for a while, and then registered a boy. They all wanted to know if I had four children. When I said "No," they asked if I had a miscarriage. I said, "No," again. We couldn't figure it out. So when I became pregnant for the fourth time, I knew it would be a boy!

Working in the office at the university, opening and closing filing cabinets was a daily task. One day, I opened more than one drawer at a time, and the filing cabinet fell on me. I struggled to push it back. The next day, I started having pain in my back and called my bosses to say I wouldn't be at work. Then I called my doctor, and he said to go to the hospital immediately as we knew I was pregnant.

My husband was at work, and I had to drive to his work. I didn't want to go to the hospital alone. His work staff called him into the office, and my husband took me to the hospital. They tried to stop the baby from coming by giving me a shot. It was so painful. Then they said they had to hope the baby would be born because it didn't stop. And I was afraid they would have to give me another shot. That was one of the births where I didn't have to make my husband a meal before we left for the hospital and came home to a sink full of dishes.

The nurses didn't watch me closely, and once when they came in, I told them I thought the baby was coming. They checked, and sure enough, the baby was coming. They pulled the bed from the room so fast that all plugs came out of the wall, lights flashing. My son was born at six and a half months and weighed just under five pounds. The doctor didn't think he was a preemie. My children were usually over eight pounds, so I knew he was a preemie. They said I had just counted wrong. Because they thought he was a full-term baby, they said we could take him home if we wanted. We decided it was best to leave him in the hospital for a few days, and it was a good thing that we did. When I called, excited about our new baby, the following day and asked how he was, they said he had stopped breathing several times during the night.

Being very religious, we questioned whether we should immediately get him baptized. We decided to wait a few days. He developed jaundice and was in the hospital for about two weeks. Each day, he got better, and we waited to get him baptized. He is now six feet tall and the tallest of my children. We baptized him later, when he was a few months old.

My son also was allergic to milk and would drink the milk down and immediately throw the whole bottle up curdled like cottage cheese. Mom had come to help me because he was so premature, and we would have a blanket or towel ready to catch the milk. The doctor couldn't tell me why he did it, and finally, I put him on non-dairy baby formula, and he was fine. Sometimes a mom knows more instinctively than a doctor.

Always wanting to be a good employee, I looked for ways to help my bosses—there were two at the University of Wisconsin, Oshkosh branch. One day, I decided to straighten their desk to make it easier to find their paperwork. I quickly learned they were unhappy, and I never did it again! They were excellent bosses and treated me very well. Over time, I realized that, in my case, male bosses were better than female bosses for me.

Winters were brutal on me as I started showing signs of arthritis. Parking was in the back of the university building, and you had to walk up the steps to get into the building. By the time I had walked up the steps, my hands and legs were stiff, and it took a while before I could type. Over time, the doctor gave me the maximum amount of medicine to stop the arthritis, but I still suffered from it. After the divorce and when we arrived in Tucson, I would lie out in the sun after work, and the heat would help my arthritis. It was years before the pain came back.

Our car was getting older, and my husband said it wasn't cost-effective to keep it. My husband purchased a stick-shift car to replace the automatic shift because he knew I couldn't drive that kind and wouldn't teach me how to drive it. Of course, *he wouldn't let me drive a car anyway, so what did it matter* (control)?

I did drive an automatic car before his sister, my best friend, had an accident. From then on, *my husband wouldn't let me take the car anymore. He said I could no longer operate a vehicle and not have an accident* (control). His mother, injured in the accident, should have gone to a doctor. However, his father said that the mother would be fine by the time she *walked to Oshkosh* (mental abuse). We were in the country, and it was several miles from town.

Because my husband would not allow me to drive, my aunt would pick me up on Fridays when she went into town. She took the baby and me to see my sister. She brought me home at the end of the day after her shopping. That was how I could get out of the house and see my sister. I had to get up early to get the baby and me ready whenever she arrived. Once, I left the stove on, and the pot was burning dry when a delivery person came to the house. I almost burned the house down.

Eventually, I was allowed to drive again when I started working. I got a job where I had to be at work "before" my husband got home. If I didn't leave before he came home from work, he would make me late because he would keep me from going on time. Whenever we had an argument and I tried just to leave to get away from him, *he would take the car keys away so I couldn't leave. There was no way to get away from him* (control).

He had complete control over anything I did or anywhere I went. We went to a Christmas party at his work every year. The men saved money all year for a great party. The women dressed up, and we had a lot of fun. I made a fancy blue taffeta long dress that I designed with a gold twisted rope trim around the waist. *He saw it and said I had to cut it short* (control). My neighbor tried to help me turn the bottom up so I wouldn't have to cut the bottom off, but the taffeta's cloth was too stiff and didn't work. I told him I couldn't cut it off and went wearing the long dress. It was a great success, and he was jealous of my attention.

CHAPTER 9

Bought Farm

After renting for a while, we bought a home on forty acres. We had a house and barn, a tractor, a car, a truck, and a couple of cows we were feeding for meat in the freezer. We raised corn on the acreage for extra income. The house was a two-story, and the upstairs wasn't heated. Our second daughter couldn't stand the cold and would cough at night, and I would have to take her downstairs. Once I had just varnished all the stairs and was hurrying to get her downstairs when I slipped and fell backward, knocking the wind out of me. I think I also broke a couple of ribs because they hurt for months. After I fell, I put the carpet in the middle of each stair. I bought samples and had coordinating colors down the stairs to save money. Each piece was one dollar, so it was reasonable to carpet the steps.

The house had no bathroom when we bought it. There also wasn't a drain in the kitchen sink. A pail caught the water when you opened the doors under the sink. The drawers had significant bite marks. When asked, the seller said the bite marks were from rats. My husband put out rat traps for days and caught lots of rats. We finally got rid of the rats.

The yard was a great distance from the road and had a ditch. It was my duty to mow the grass. Being pregnant with the third child, I could no longer cut the grass. When my husband had to mow the grass, *he promptly purchased a ride-on mower!*

The house was a two-story with bedrooms upstairs, and because the upstairs wasn't heated, I put lots of blankets on the kids in the winter to keep them warm. Along with the extra blankets, the kids had warm pajamas. I would buy a large blanket on sale and use it to make pajamas. It was the kind where they would put their arms and feet in and zip up the front, and they were all snuggly and warm. I could make several pajamas out of one blanket. I would also cut down an adult coat for winter to make a child's coat. The kids were always in nice outfits that cost little money.

By now, we had three children. We never did get heat in the upstairs. Our daughter finally outgrew the problem of coughing at night; of course, the Tucson weather was great for her.

My husband built a bathroom onto the back of the house, but there was no heating in that room either, so pipes froze up during the winter when we wanted to take a bath. One night, I was taking a bath, and we had just gotten over a fight. He tried to make up for sex. I was in no mood for loving and stayed in the bath. *He came up to me, pinched, and twisted my nipple because he was so upset.* Other times, *he would pull me by my hair around the house* (physical abuse). *If he were yelling at me, he would follow me from room to room so that I could hear every abusive word. I couldn't get away from him* (mental abuse). *He took the car keys away if I tried to drive away in the car* (control). It was hard to remember that this man claimed to love me!

I wanted a backsplash of tile on the wall behind the washbasin in the new bathroom and had no one to put it in. The men at the lumberyard helped me. They showed me square foot sheets with one-inch tiles on sheets of fabric backing with slots between the tiles. They sold me some pliers to cut the sheets to fit the plumbing, and my oldest son and I put up the tile and the grout between the tiles. It was a professional job, if I didn't say so myself.

My husband's father would give us a calf or two to raise for meat. We had a large freezer and kept it full of beef, pork, chicken, vegetables, and the bakery I made. Our cow got out of the barn a few times. Being a city girl, I didn't know how to chase a cow. I chased it from behind, and it headed straight ahead to the main road. I caught up with it once and had my hands around its neck. I yelled to my husband, "Come and get it. I have it." My husband had a fit because the cow could have kicked me. He had to explain to me how to chase a cow. If you don't know, you get in front of it and turn it around so it heads back to the barn. Another lesson the city girl learned.

My husband started putting in cement for the foundation for a large corncrib. The cement surface still had to be smoothed when he got a call that he had to go to work. I had to help the others finish the cement—the city girl. It made me feel good that I could do it.

We raised a few cattle in the barn to slaughter for meat in the freezer. There was a well near the barn that needed repairing. Instead of getting it fixed, *my husband made my son carry water from the basement to the barn for the cows. He was about nine or ten at that time. He had to make the trip many times to have enough water for the cows* (control). My husband didn't want to spend the money to fix the well, so our son had to carry the water. According to my husband, taking the water wasn't a punishment, just a chore.

We drove into the yard one day, and my husband said the windows upstairs looked dirty. *He wanted to know why I didn't wash the outside because he could see they were filthy* (control). It was never, "Let me help you." It was always presumed to be the "woman's job." I don't know how he thought I was supposed to clean the outside of the upstairs windows.

My husband also thought there was no reason I shouldn't scrape the outside of the house and paint it (control). The house was made of wood slate, and the paint was very chipped. He made a tool of a rod and sickle blade, which I used to scrape the side of the house. After that, I had to paint it. Remember, this was a two-story house! I did just the sides damaged by the weather. That was when I learned I could do anything. I wasn't stupid, lazy, "couldn't do that," or any of the other abusive words my husband repeatedly told me.

My oldest son was only about ten years old when I painted the two-story stairwell walls, and he was sure his mom was going to break her neck. I had a ladder on boxes on the stairs to paint the walls up to the ceiling. The walls were dirty, and there was no one else to do it, so he held the ladder, and I painted. Neither of us fell during this remodeling project! I don't believe I would try it again.

I always told the kids we all had angels on our shoulders to watch over us, and the angels had a *big* job! We usually did crazy things because we had to—there was no one else to do it! The boxes and ladder stayed put, and all went well. I was about twenty-seven at the time. It was pretty crazy when you looked back on it!

One day, I was in the basement doing laundry, and the kids were upstairs playing with my oldest son's rabbit. They were in a chair, and my youngest daughter held the rabbit. All at once, I heard a loud noise that sounded like one of the kids was in trouble, and I yelled upstairs to see what was happening. My oldest son called back that my youngest daughter was making a funny noise and shaking. When I ran upstairs, it looked like she was having convulsions.

Doctors still made house calls in those days and said he would be right out. Being in the country, it would take a while. By the time the doctor arrived, my husband was home from work. My husband started yelling at me *that our daughter was filthy as she was ashen colored and wanted to know when the last time was that I had washed her* (mental abuse). Because of her temperature and because she was sick, she was that gray, but he just took it out on me as if I were lazy and it was my fault and that she was ill. His discussion was all said to me outside the doctor's hearing. The doctor decided she was allergic to the rabbit, and she came out of it. It didn't happen again.

My husband once abused me, and I called the police. I wanted a record on file in case something happened to me. Having the abuse on record could save you in the future. My youngest daughter remembered that and asked me about it recently. She said she was excited to see the police and opened the door for him. My husband saw it was the police and told her to get upstairs. This was before the days when they separated the two fighting spouses. She said she was scared of her father when he ordered her upstairs.

Allergies ran in my family. My dad had allergies bad enough to move to another state. I had allergies, and two of our four children had allergies. We didn't know that our oldest daughter was allergic to horses.

We got a pony for the kids, and they named it Sugar. Our daughter loved going out, rubbing her face against Sugar, and loving on the pony. Her face got rashes and swelled, and she had to stop "loving" Sugar. The kids could all ride the pony very safely. But if an adult got on the pony, it would head straight for the barn door and try to throw the adult off. One day, we had company, and the kid's uncle, tall with long legs, said, "Let me ride that pony. I will show him who's boss." He got on Sugar and wrapped his legs around the belly, and the pony trotted right for the barn. We all laughed as the pony showed the uncle who was boss. Adults didn't try to ride the pony after that. Because of our daughter's allergies, we finally had to get rid of Sugar.

The kids and I also put shelves in their closets for all their toys. It was a big, long closet with lots of shelf space. I measured the length and width of the wood needed and went to the store. Having no way to cut the boards to size myself, I asked the men if they would cut the lengths for me, and they were kind enough to do it. They told me what kind of brackets to use and nails or whatever to attach the boards to the wall. The shelves looked very professional when done. It is incredible what you can do when you have no one else to do it and want something done.

My oldest son and I learned to do some amazing things. He was my regular little carpenter. His wife has a rental business now, and he helps with all the upkeep, renovations, and repairs. He is also an excellent photographer and could sell professionally.

My friend had given me two geese to raise so I could have them for meat. They were supposed to be friendly and be friendly to me, but they didn't know that. Every time I stepped out the back door, they would chase me to the barn, biting at my feet. They were the most vicious geese I had ever seen. They sure got up on the wrong side of the hay every day. I was so glad to see them go into the freezer.

My mother-in-law helped me butcher the chickens and the geese because I was a city girl and didn't know the first thing about cutting the heads off of a chicken. By this time, we were great friends. She was such a thoughtful person. She knew what I was going through but couldn't help me. So she cut the heads off, and we plucked the feathers and got the birds ready for the freezers.

She raised big chickens as big as small turkeys, which were so good. My father-in-law bought her chicks every spring. That was how she received her spending money. She earned her spending money by selling chickens and eggs. She didn't have money either. Like father, like son!

My mom and dad would come about once a year to see us. It was always tense when they were with me as my husband was jealous of the attention. One time, my dad heard about my husband physically abusing me and suggested that my husband go outside and fight with a man instead of a woman. My husband never left the house. In desperation, my dad went down to see my husband's dad. The dad said our life was none of their business, and that was that. My dad was furious. He didn't know what to do to help his daughter—me.

When my husband and I got divorced, I was supposed to get the house, and he got everything else. Then my husband changed his mind. He said I should receive about thirty acres and not the house—we had a forty-acre piece of property. He finally settled on the figure I was to get: twenty-four acres and nothing else but the car and furniture I could take to Tucson. We didn't have lawyers, only the judge to decide the divorce settlement. The judge didn't even ask me if the payment was okay. He didn't question how unfair it was. My child support was fifty dollars per child per month, or two hundred dollars a month for all four.

I was traumatized at the time and didn't realize we had much more. For example, we must have had a bank account. I forgot that we had farm equipment, land planted with corn, cattle in the barn, snowmobiles, and on and on. He got everything not mentioned in the divorce! Now the wife receives part of the retirement account.

Why didn't I fight for more? Because my support system was all in Tucson. I feared his family would get involved, and I would get even less. I believed his family was already part of the divorce dealings, and I was scared things would worsen, so I accepted without question. My childcare in Tucson was two hundred dollars a month—what I received for child support *if* I got it.

I have always believed that if you and your partner have decided to move on in life alone, each should be treated fairly in the property division so that each could build a new life. That did not happen in my divorce! I see it in many divorces; usually, the woman takes the hit.

I wrote to the University of Arizona campus when we were getting ready to move to Tucson. I was working at the University of Wisconsin Oshkosh campus and thought they might have a position for me in Tucson. The University in Oshkosh paid well, and I presumed that any university also paid well. How wrong I was. My bosses gave me a good recommendation, and there were positions ready to apply for when the kids and I got to Tucson.

Notice I got divorced and moved two thousand miles away. I could do that because my family lived in Tucson, Arizona. If I had not moved, I am sure he would have convinced me to go back to him. If you can move a distance away, it is always better—that way, your ex cannot find you and harass you. That might not be possible today, but I would fight to move based on the abuse.

CHAPTER 10

Divorce and Moving to Tucson

After the divorce, the kids and I moved to Tucson to be with my family. When we left Wisconsin, I was thirty-one years old. The kids were thirteen, twelve, eight, and one. The kids had to depend on me for their food, clothes, and a roof over their heads, starting with new friends and a new school and trusting that I could do it all. They never questioned my ability to do it. We never discussed it. We all accepted that I could and would care for all of us! I have had much help from family, friends, and my religion.

My family said they could help care for the kids while I worked. At first, until we found an apartment, we would stay with my mom and stepdad, who had only been married about a year. Five people moving into their three-bedroom home was quite a disruption, but they were willing to live with it to help me.

I planned to drive the kids to Tucson myself. In theory, this was an excellent plan; however, I wasn't good at directions and invariably turned in the opposite direction when I needed to change directions. Also, having been told for several years by my husband that I wasn't allowed to drive and, "Why would I think I could do this?" it was a terrible idea. My mom, bless her heart, decided there was no way she was allowing me to drive to Tucson with the kids.

She arranged for my brother to fly to Oshkosh and drive us all out. Now my brother was a police officer in Tucson. They are to always have their guns on them. With my husband being as abusive to me as he was, my brother decided it was in everyone's best interest that my brother not have a gun in his possession when he picked me up. Things were agitated as my husband did not want the divorce and did not want me to take the children out of state. I could only take them out of Wisconsin because it benefited my health. Nowadays, that would not be allowed. I don't know what I would have done because my entire support system was in Tucson.

My brother stayed at a motel overnight and took a taxi to pick the kids and me up in the morning. My husband tried to convince me to stay. It was touch-and-go because I had always given in to him. I told him I was leaving and he could come with us. He didn't want to do that. This time, I was brave and left. I received the Chevy convertible in the divorce, and that is what we took to Tucson. It was raining very hard when we left, and the rain came through around the convertible windows like there were no windows. We had blankets up to the windows and anything else to stop the water from coming in.

On the trip, we also had a slight problem with my baby! He was allergic to milk, and I had to give him milk on the trip. He had tummy problems. Every time I fed him, he would "toot," giggle, and laugh out loud. The gas smell was unbelievable. We just burst out laughing every time he drank his milk. Thank heavens he didn't get stomach cramps, as that would have been difficult for me to bear. It was bad enough that he had to drink regular milk.

It made a bad situation bearable when we could laugh. My brother never had such a trip as ours. He sure loved his sister to do what he did on that trip. We missed a turnoff at one point. Crossing a median to go in the other direction was illegal, and my brother went several miles out of the way so we could turn around. Being a police officer, he followed all the rules. He didn't want to get a ticket!

When we stopped at night, they didn't believe a brother was driving his sister and her kids to Tucson, so they put him on one end of the motel and me and the kids on the other. It was funny to think they were protecting someone—*who?* We looked at each other and shook our heads. Now, people were trying to protect me!

We had to dry and air out the car when we got to Tucson! The rain and my baby's tummy problems had left their marks. It was August 1972 when we arrived in Tucson in time to put the kids in school.

Friends asked if I got counseling after the abuse; unfortunately, I did not. It did not occur to me. My time was constantly focused on how the kids and I would make it. That is all I thought of. In hindsight, *counseling should have been the first thing I did* after getting divorced and away from the abuse. I encourage you to get counseling. Money was an issue for me; however, there must be organizations that would have helped me get counseling either for free or at a reduced cost. Please check it out for yourself. Even today, I realize how much it would have helped me and the kids.

Within a week of reaching Tucson, I had a job. The recommendation from the university in Wisconsin had helped. The wages for a clerk in Wisconsin were very high compared to a clerk in Tucson at the university. It was quite a difference in pay, and it took forever to get the first paycheck. It took six weeks for the system to catch up with their schedule. When you have little or no money, waiting every week with no compensation is frightening. It was getting quite severe before the check finally came through. Each payday, I would ask if there was a check for me. Each payday, they would say, "No." Finally, they said, "Yes!"

On top of the lack of a paycheck, our furniture took forever to arrive. When it finally did reach Tucson, I wasn't home, and the truckers started unloading the furniture on the sidewalk.

We've made it. We are all free! What a wonderful feeling, and we are getting used to the five of us being on our own. Everyone pitched in to make this work. My oldest son took it upon himself to be the "man of the house" by ensuring everything and everyone was okay. He was thirteen at the time. He even went so far as to look out for families at school. One time, I mentioned Easter. He thought I was asking him to help me. He said, "Mom, I am helping buy Easter things for this family at school because the mom just couldn't." I explained that I wasn't asking for help and said I was saying Easter was coming up. His response made me feel like we were "doing okay" as a family. I was so proud that he was helping others in need. He was a very responsible thirteen-year-old.

Freedom in Tucson was intoxicating after years of abuse. I would leave work at 5:00 p.m. and get in the car. First, I would open the convertible top and drive home smiling. As I went down the street with the top down, young men in other cars would flirt with me. I remember thinking, If only they knew I had four kids. It made me feel good to have positive attention.

Only my sister knew of my problem getting my paycheck. My sister asked my mom if she had talked with me lately about my pay. My mom said, "No, what's wrong?" I did not feel comfortable asking family for help and was on my last ten dollars when the check came through. My mom yelled at me for not telling her, mainly because I had four kids to feed. Mom always thought of us before herself. If she had money and thought we needed it, she would give us the "shirt off her back," as they say. My mom was not well-off by any means. She also worked as a clerk at the University of Arizona and was paid a low income until the day she retired. She worked there for years and never was promoted. Her duties were well above her pay scale.

My sister was taking care of all four children then, so I didn't have to pay for childcare. I would take the kids to her house, and the three oldest walked to school with her four children. The school was less than a block away. The baby stayed home with my sister.

The kids came home from school for lunch because it was so close. My youngest daughter would only eat Franco-American SpaghettiOs (she says she still does), and my sister was worried she would get malnourished. My sister babysat the kids until her husband said she couldn't anymore. His idea of divorced women was terrible! He felt they just ran around looking for men. That's hard to do with four children! He believed it was costing them too much money to continue helping me. My sister was devastated. She couldn't believe what he thought of me. She knew I was working hard and didn't have time to run around. She knew how much her care for the children helped me, and she was embarrassed to tell me she could no longer take care of the kids.

It wasn't easy to find a place that would take an infant. They all wanted the child to be potty trained. After my sister couldn't babysit anymore, I found a church that took in babies that weren't potty trained and left my youngest there on the way to work. He would scream while I walked up to the door and back to the car. That is hard on a mother. I cried all the way back to the car. The woman at the daycare said he stopped crying when I left, but that didn't help. You could smell dirty diapers when you walked through the front door of the daycare. But I had no choice because I needed a place that would take a baby.

Later, I found a better daycare with a church that was closer to home and more reasonably priced. It even smelled good! He stayed there until he entered school. I remember thinking I could purchase a car with the money I saved from childcare when he went to school. Childcare is even worse for parents today. My heart goes out to the parents.

My first job at the university was typing letters and other correspondence from recordings. The accents gave me a little trouble, especially when I heard the city of Tempe and thought it was 10P. The whole letter had "10P" instead of the city of Tempe. The staff, at first, couldn't figure out why I had typed 10P. Then they explained that it was the city of Tempe. I also had trouble with the name Jesus. They would say, "Heysouse," and I didn't know how to spell it. When they spelled it for me, I said, "Oh, you mean Jesus!"

While working at the university, I also typed a statistical booklet for the computer staff's research project. We had no computers, and I worked on a typewriter then. Make a mistake, and you start over. When the team changed the figures, I typed the document over. Before I completed the paper, they were already changing what I was typing. It took forever to get a completed manuscript, and there was much statistical typing for a "clerk." There were many charts. My job was as a clerk, not a secretary, which is another reason my pay was low.

It was early in my move, and my birthday came around. It wasn't a happy time to think of sitting home and celebrating alone. I asked one of the men at work I liked if he would go out with me for my birthday so I wouldn't have to spend it alone. He agreed, and we went out and had a good time. We didn't go out again. The thought of my four children probably had something to do with it, and I sure don't blame anyone. That was never an issue with me. I always expected to raise the children on my paycheck and not expect the man to pay for them.

My birthday has been a big problem for me because of my marriage. My ex did not think there was any reason to celebrate anything for me. I only wanted to know that my husband loved me enough to remember. He didn't. I still get very depressed for two weeks before my birthday, and it is hard on the kids because they don't always have it on their calendars or get busy and forget to celebrate. They always call to wish me a happy birthday, but I need a celebration. I still need to know that I "am loved." It is an unfortunate time for me around my birthday. It doesn't get better as time goes on.

When my kids were younger, they waited until Mother's Day and were going to get me flowers on the way to church. They hadn't given me anything yet. As we passed people selling flowers by the side of the road, my oldest asked me to stop so he could buy me flowers. I told them, "If they didn't have time to get me something before, they didn't have to get it now!" I was upset that they had waited until Mother's Day to get something. It was quiet in the car!

Mom looked for an apartment while I went to work the first week. She found an apartment for us right away. We had to have a three-bedroom apartment because I had two boys and two girls, and by law, the boys had to have their bedroom, the girls had to have their bedroom, and I had to have my own.

The apartment Mom found was just off Davis Monthan's airbase. It had the usual accessories, like a pool and laundry. We would take our laundry out and put it in the washing machines, go back to our apartment, and an hour later go back and put them in the dryers. We would go home and come back to fold them once they were dry.

Once, when I went back for the clothes, they weren't there. Someone had stolen them.

The apartment is where the children learned to swim. They taught themselves when they saw the other kids having so much fun. I never learned to swim. I am afraid of being in the water.

I was very lonely in the apartment, the sole person responsible for four young children and me at age thirty-one. One night in the kitchen, I said, "Lord, I am so lonely."

I felt a hug go around me. It sounded as if someone said, "I am always here for you." It was very comforting. Yes, I believe in a higher power! I was comforted.

My youngest child was just a baby, and the other kids were in school. I went into the apartment's backyard for something, and the baby shut the door. It automatically locks upon closing. I didn't know this. The baby was inside, and there was no way for me to get in. I had to go to the office and have them let me in the apartment. That wasn't very comforting to have your baby inside and not be able to get in. Big lesson: always have a key to the apartment on you.

Months after moving into the apartment, we discovered the maintenance man had keys to all our apartments twenty-four seven, and we started finding things missing. Neighbors told us the maintenance man would wear a long coverall. That made it easy to steal anything he could hide under the covering, such as watches, cameras, jewelry, and anything small and worth money. He had a U-Haul in front of his apartment for months. We couldn't figure out why.

When we started finding our things missing and called the police, we knew where our things had gone. I had my diamond wedding rings, class ring, watches, cameras, and other small items stolen. By then, the maintenance man and the U-Haul were gone. The police told us to confront the manager, and when we did, he said there was nothing wrong with the maintenance man, his friend, having keys to our apartments twenty-four seven. We tried to explain and got nowhere. We just lost anything valuable that was small. Our cases went unsolved.

Most people living in apartments don't have insurance on their furnishings as it is costly, so we didn't get any reimbursement. By that time, I had nothing worthwhile left anyway. At first, I tried to get insurance, and the agent said there was no way I would be approved because I was divorced. He said most divorced people put their money into expensive stereos and other furnishings. My insurance agent convinced the company that I was a single mom with four children and had nothing worthwhile left. They finally insured me.

Around this time, I walked out the door to work, and the car wouldn't start. The neighbor was always willing to help me, so I went to see what he could do. As a single mom with four kids, neighbors were ready to help me, and I was so grateful for the help. Anyway, he opened the hood and said, "Sandy, didn't you have a die-hard battery?"

Being a woman, I was lucky to know there was a battery in the car, so I said, "I have no idea."

He said, "I'm sure you did, and this is an old clunker." Someone had taken my battery out and put a different one in its place. At least, they put a battery in. I didn't realize it until it failed. I was beginning to think Tucson didn't want us to be here and that we should go home. The neighbor changed the battery to a good one again, and of course, we stayed. My family was here!

While in the apartment, I went to the neighbor's left of our apartment, a young couple with no children lived there. I had a problem and wanted their help or advice. They knew I worked at the police department by this time and were smoking marijuana. They said I sniffed around and were scared I'd tell the police. To be truthful, I was too naïve and didn't know the smell. They helped me, and I went home none the wiser about what they were doing.

During my first years in Tucson, a reporter from the newspaper contacted me, and they wanted to do a story on my life as an abused person. I don't know how this came about—if I called them or they called me—but since my experiences, it has been vital to me to help others out of an abusive situation or realize it before marriage. The reporter came over several times to get my story. She told me she knew what I was talking about and understood because she also had been abused.

It seems like I can speak with women and find out that many are also in abusive relationships. I don't know the percentage of abusive relationships, but in my discussions, it appears to be about 25 percent. That is a high percentage!

The reporter turned the completed report over to her editor. She came over to see me later and was very upset. As my story unfolded, her male editor refused to print the story. He said he didn't believe it would take years to recover from an abusive relationship. Both she and I were very discouraged by his decision. Indeed, he didn't know anyone who had been through it. It occurred to me that perhaps he was an abuser and didn't want to believe the recovery took so long. If you have not walked in the abused shoes, don't decide how long healing takes. Sometimes the abused are brainwashed, and it could take years to believe in themselves again.

Just as my sister, brother, and I loved pets when we were little, my kids were the same. If I had to leave for a day or so, invariably, I would come home to a new dog or cat "that followed them home." It was hard for my oldest son to use that excuse when he held a cat in his arms while riding a bike. I tried to explain that to him, but he insisted the cat was lost and he saved it. Right!

The kids convinced me to let them have rabbits. My oldest son had a rabbit in Wisconsin, and he loved it. I figured rabbits couldn't be too difficult to raise and said, "Yes." They wanted two, and the clerk at the store said both were the same sex, so we wouldn't have to worry about babies. Oh, how little they knew! The next thing, little black things, fell through the cage to the ground. Yup! Baby bunnies. I guess the store clerk couldn't tell the sexes of the bunnies. That was fun. Now, we had several bunnies to feed. The kids were thrilled because they now all had at least one bunny.

Over time, the kids had gerbils, guinea pigs, cats, dogs, a rat, and even an iguana. At first, I didn't know we had an iguana in the house because my youngest son kept it in his room. When he purchased the iguana, it was only my youngest son and me at home. When I finally saw it, I was upset. This pet was the ugliest I had ever seen and resided in my house! My son convinced me it could not get out of its enclosure. Did you hear the phrase "famous last words?"

It got out, and he didn't know where it was and didn't tell me it was running about the house.

Eventually, I became aware that the animal was roaming the house. I convinced myself that I could hear it in my bathroom at night. Or so I thought! I would yell to him to come and get his animal. For several nights, I thought I heard this animal. He never found the iguana in my bathroom. He finally found it hanging on the top of my drapes in the living room, looking down on us! That iguana and the rat were the only "pets" I didn't like.

I was always short on money because I didn't get the child support check on time. The trick with the child support was for him to pay it on time. It didn't happen. It was always late, and we needed it to live. My ex-husband had an excellent job, so there was no issue with money. He didn't want us—or me—to have it. He found a way to pay child support without "actually paying child support!" Now that is quite a trick.

Before the divorce, a renter had crops on our land. My ex had put it in the divorce that he was to collect the money to pay the property taxes and anything else during the last year of our marriage. *After the divorce, my ex continued collecting rent on my land* (control). He would cash the check my ex asked the renter to write out to *him*, and he sent the payment with *his name* through the child support court. The court credited it as his child support. He was paying child support with my money!

It took me a while to figure out what he was doing, and by that time, it was too late because the court didn't believe me when I explained. There was no way to prove it. So *he got away with paying child support with money owed to me* for the land rented by someone else (control). That continued until I sold the property. Great guy! I figured that, in reality, he owed me thousands of dollars in back child support, which I had no way of ever receiving. It is a sore spot to this day.

It was summer, a few years after we moved to Tucson, and my oldest son wanted to visit his dad in Oshkosh. My ex agreed to pay for the trip as it was in the divorce degree that he was responsible for the kids going back and forth to see him, he again sent the money through the court *to come off his child support payments* (control). Furthermore, he was using the money he agreed to pay for the trip to pay his child support. The airline ticket money became child support. I paid for the trip!

While my oldest son was there, *he had to watch his father burn the toys we left behind and any other things we cherished. My ex burned my high school yearbooks* (mental abuse), and I was devastated when I heard. One of my high school classmates sent me three years of his yearbooks when he heard how I had lost mine. We talked, and I found out his ex-wife abused him. I hadn't realized women beat or controlled men! I was so grateful that he had sent the books. They were so precious to me. I could now look back and see my high school years.

When each child turned eighteen, my ex would write a letter saying he was no longer covering their health insurance. These letters hurt the kids. In reality, it wasn't costing him anything to keep our kids on his policy as he was already covering one child at home. I had to add the kids to my policy.

It saddened me also because my ex didn't acknowledge the kids on their birthdays or Christmas. He didn't contact them by letter, telephone, or send a gift. He just ignored them because it was "easier for him." However, it wasn't easy for our kids. They felt abandoned. When the boys returned to Wisconsin, he told the kids what he and his wife bought for the new daughter for Christmas and birthdays. It was always a large item, such as a snowmobile. He always bragged to them about how much money he had. The kids knew how we had to live but said nothing. They accepted that as the way their father was. Of course, I had a *big* problem with it!

Years later, he contacted the oldest boy occasionally by telephone. My ex told my oldest son he hadn't included the kids in his will and asked him to advise the rest.

When my ex-husband's father passed away, my oldest son returned for the funeral because he remembered his grandpa the most and could afford the trip. People back east didn't recognize my son. They hadn't seen him for so long and soon realized who he was and included him in the group.

Their grandfather included all his grandchildren in his will. He gave $500 to each grandchild, including our children, yet their father does not have our four in his will. I don't want this to sound like our children think this is terrible. They think nothing of it and accept it. Their mother, me, thinks it is not good! I realize that people have the right to do whatever they want with their will; however, you should include all your children if you include one child. That is why I have said if you remarry, include your first children in your memories and treat all the children the same if you marry again. They are still a part of your "family." They remember and love you.

Our four children have given their father ten grandchildren and five great-grandchildren. They all live in Tucson. He has never seen any of them or had the pleasure of knowing them. How sad!

Money was so tight during this time that I had three credit cards. I would use a credit card if I didn't have money for a bill. Sometimes I used one credit card to pay for the other credit card. It is the only way I could stay ahead of the game. I usually only paid the minimum payment. It was a scary time. It was several years before I could start paying the cards off. Today we are debt-free! Take heart; you can do it too.

As a freshly divorced person with little money, the washing machine broke early in my young life. There was no money to get it fixed or a new one, so I discussed this "with the Lord." I talk to him like I talk to anyone. My sister tells me to pray instead of her because the Lord knows and hears me! Anyway, the washer started working again. I don't know if it fixed itself or if the Lord had something to do with it. You judge.

Three times this happened; finally, I said, "Okay, Lord, I can handle this now." I went out and bought a new washing machine. The kids just shook their heads. We did have fun and tried to make things happy. My oldest son recently commented that he is glad I didn't get bitter with men.

My youngest son has often told me he is grateful and, "You got us out of there when you did." He was too young to see or be a part of the abuse. If I mention something that happened back then and ask him about it, he says, "Mom, I wasn't there." I will then remember that he wasn't, and I am so glad!

My paycheck went into the bank two days before payday because of the City of Tucson's system. That gave me an extra two days to get bills in the mail and pay them. Sometimes, the money wasn't there, and I would receive notice that they would shut off the electricity. I would then have to send my oldest son downtown to pay the bill in person. He didn't like that chore! Sometimes, I couldn't help it. He always went but wasn't happy.

We couldn't afford much for Christmas, so I would get the kids' little things and wrap them. About a week before Christmas, I would start putting out little notes around the house. Each day was something different: "Santa says, 'Look in the dryer.' Santa says, "Look on top of the refrigerator.'" They would have to look in several places until they found the gift. The gifts were things for the girl's hair or something the boys would like. Sometimes, it was things for school. They got a kick out of it, and it was a cheap way for me to add to their Christmas fun.

During the late fall, about three or four months before Christmas, I would try to find extra work so we could have a good Christmas. One year, I was invited to a Christmas Around the World by House of Lloyd party and thought, *Hey, this is something I would like to do as I liked Christmas so much.* I talked with the demonstrator and liked what I heard. They signed me up, and I worked that first Christmas. In addition to the parties to earn money, we could sign up schools, churches, and other groups to sell fundraiser items. The groups could make some good income from the fundraisers, we earned a percentage, and it helped us earn trips, which I learned about later.

In January, my director called to see if I also wanted to work in the spring. That sounded pretty good to have extra income year-round. She explained what was involved: I would have to do the *Cooking the American Way* parties in the spring and then the Christmas parties in the fall. I love cooking but wasn't into doing cooking parties. After thinking it over and realizing it would provide extra income in the spring, I decided to try it. Some promotions went along with this, and this was the first time I realized we could earn free trips to places outside the continental United States, such as Hawaii, Alaska, London, and Germany, to name a few. That sounded especially exciting as there was no way I could ever afford such trips.

By working the first full year, I made a couple extra thousand dollars a year, which came in handy. They offered to promote me to supervisor the following year if I hired and trained other women. If I get into something, I am always thinking about how I could make this "an even better proposition." Being a supervisor sounded pretty good, and I started advertising and recruiting a team. The company offered advertising money to help us out. People could start by having five parties booked, and the company gave them a tool kit of products worth $300. No money was involved, which made it very easy to recruit. They earned the sales kits from the five parties and usually continued working. We started our little group. My district manager lived in California, where I had to attend the training.

After working several years, I finally made enough money to get the two youngest kids *new* bikes, not used bikes. The older ones had already left home. The two youngest were older when they got bikes, just like my siblings and me. Here is a warning: "Don't ask your kids what color they want." My youngest daughter wanted a blue bike. Have you ever tried to find a blue lady's bike? Only men's bikes are blue. It took quite a while before I finally found a blue bike. I was getting a little worried for a while.

The kids enjoyed their bikes so much. It was the way my younger son got to work at night. One night he had already closed out when the business started getting busy, and he decided to go back in and help them. He left his bike outside and went in to help. When he came out, the bike was gone. He had to call me to go and get him. He never found his bike.

The year when Cabbage Patch dolls just came out in the 1980s, I decided I wanted one. They were so different and ugly that I just had to have one. Remember that I love dolls. The kids couldn't believe I wanted one but started looking for one. They were so popular that they were hard enough to find for the little girls—say nothing about one for moms. My youngest daughter found one and had it wrapped on Christmas morning. I had opened all the gifts but no Cabbage Patch doll. I made her believe I was sad, pouting, lip down, the whole bit. Finally, they brought out another package—*the* doll! It was such a hit. I still have it on a shelf. It has adoption papers and all.

CHAPTER 11

Sale of Land, Bought First Home

As for the twenty-four acres I received in the divorce settlement, I never remember signing paperwork to put the property in my name, receiving property tax bills, or signing papers when I sold the property.

Years later, I realized that my ex probably never had my name on the property, home, and land, to begin with, and *never put the twenty-four acres in my name when we divorced. On paper, I don't believe I ever really owned anything except in the divorce papers* (control)!

The only way that could have happened is if my ex went to the person who rented the land, asked that a check be made out to him, which he cashed, and sent me the payment with *his* check through the child support court. *I don't know how much I rented or sold the land for—only what my ex sent me! I had no paper trail, signed or otherwise. I don't even know the name of the person renting and eventually buying the land so that I could check with them* (control). I trusted him to do the right thing, and he didn't. A hard lesson learned too late to correct.

The year the renter bought the land, my ex had already sent the rent money through the court, and I had to send the money back to the renter. My ex handled the return of the rent money as I didn't know to whom to send the money. Wasn't that handy for my ex? *My ex paid his child support with my money, and I had to return the money* (control). You are probably saying, "This woman was crazy to trust him!" You are right!

To finally get my ex to pay child support regularly, I had to hire two lawyers, one in Tucson and one in Wisconsin, because the divorce was in Wisconsin. *He would agree to a date to meet in court in Wisconsin. I would get an airline ticket, and he would change the date. That happened at least twice* (control). The last time the attorneys said they could do it without me being present.

How did I pay for two attorneys on a limited budget? I took a vacation from the city and worked for the Pima County Elections Department. Because it was my city vacation time, the city insisted that the county pay my city wages. I made the same high salary. Working the two weeks plus overtime gave me enough to pay the attorneys. I did this for several years and gained experience I could use later in my city job. It also gave me extra income when I didn't get child support.

I told my attorney in Wisconsin to ask for "cost of living raises." The attorney said he had never heard of that.

I was so upset by being ripped off so often that I said, "That's okay, try it." He did, and I *got it*. My ex insisted that it always go back to the beginning amount, but I got cost of living raises until my youngest turned eighteen. He had to increase the payments every two years. In the end, he was paying over three hundred dollars for one child instead of fifty dollars. I felt proud of myself for finally getting one over on him. If you find yourself abused, stick up for yourself! *But do this only after you get out.* Otherwise, you might get beaten up even more.

Grocery shopping was a new experience in Tucson. We had no taxes on food in Wisconsin. In Tucson, as I bought groceries, I kept track of the money to have enough at the checkout. Then they would add the taxes, and I would have to put some of the food back. It was so embarrassing and hard for me to remember that at first. I had to worry too much about money and how I would ever pay for everything.

Don't be afraid to question a bill if the prices go up. I call every time our paper, cable, or statement doesn't have a legitimate explanation for the price increase. We have saved a lot of money by doing so. For example, the newspaper went up by about eleven dollars a month without cause. I called to see why. She couldn't explain why the bill had increased. She also said they should have notified us of the increase. Therefore, she changed the account back to what it was before.

We save money every time the cable bill goes up. I call, and they put it back down because we have been with them for so long. If you say you will go to another cable company, they will work with you.

When you order over the internet and there is a block for a coupon code, don't ignore it if you don't have one. Click on it, and usually, a code key or series of codes will appear. You can also get savings codes from the Capital One shopping app. Look into all these codes. It pays to check those things out. There is also an app called Rakuten. Just go to https://www.rakuten.com and sign up. I have saved over $500 since joining. You get money back when you shop at stores like Safeway, CVS, or catalog companies. We have saved hundreds of dollars by questioning our bills and using codes. Every dollar saved is terrific.

Because of the lesson I learned from how my husband treated me with money in our marriage, I am always aware of what people are charging me and if I am getting my money's worth. I get upset if I believe someone is taking advantage of me.

I usually didn't have much or any money in my purse. That way, I knew that I wouldn't spend it. If mom came over to see us and I left the room for anything, she quickly checked my purse to see if I had any money, especially since it took so long to get my first paycheck, and I didn't tell her. Usually, I didn't have money in my wallet. If she could sneak a twenty in before I got back from where I had disappeared, she would try it. I told her I insisted on paying her back, and if I didn't have the money when she put the twenty in, it would be just as difficult for me to pay later. So please don't do that. She tried to honor my wishes, but sometimes she couldn't help herself, and I would find an extra twenty in the purse. But she tried to do as I asked.

While dating a man, we got an invitation to hear about a vacation opportunity. The place was called "The Ranch." It was just in the development stage. We sat on straw bales to watch the presentation. There was nothing built yet, and the price was reasonable. It sounded like a good investment, and I borrowed money from the credit union to join. There were to be horses for trail riding, a horseshoe-shaped pool, wooden cabins, dancing, and all sorts of fun stuff to do on vacation.

For several years, we went up a couple of times a year. We were able to take family and friends, which we did when they could go with us. It was always exciting to drive through the entrance, built like a ranch driveway. There was an office where you could stop on your way in and get keys to your cabin.

The kids loved riding the horses and living in the cabins. It was rustic and relaxing. We were able to enjoy "The Ranch" for several years until they started putting money into a recreational place in Florida using money earmarked for The Ranch. The Ranch was getting run down, and they no longer brought the horses from the stables for horseback riding. Little by little, the owners didn't repair the property, and the place lost its appeal.

Finally, all owners received a letter saying they were going bankrupt and would offer us money to close our account. We had no choice but to take the money offered. By now, the place was nothing like it was in its heyday. It was sad because we all enjoyed the property.

The kids and I didn't have much for Christmas. We had a used fake tree from my sister and no ornaments or lights to put on it. We found pinecones and used them as ornaments. Since then, every tree has at least one pinecone to remind us of our beginning in Tucson. I'm sure there are still a couple of pinecones in the Christmas ornament box in the garage.

We had a fake Christmas tree because I was allergic to pine needles. One year the kids talked me into getting a "real" tree and promised to water it so I didn't have to put my face in the tree. That didn't last long as "mom" had to water the tree. That was the last real tree we bought.

As Christmastime approached, the cold and wind of Tucson came in, making my migraines worse. When the wind hits my ears, it creates migraines. When I would go out, I would wear earmuffs to protect my ears. Mom had company from Wisconsin one day when I showed up with earmuffs, and they had a big laugh over my earmuffs in Tucson. You have to do what you have to do!

I sold the land I received in the divorce settlement and put the money in a CD until we could purchase a home. My mom had some money in CDs and said the interest rate was high. At the time, CDs were earning 16–17 percent interest. According to the internet, CDs in 1980 made an 18.65 percent return on a three-month CD. That is unheard of today, but it was great back then. I bought a house two years later, but the CD wasn't ready to be cashed. If I cashed in the CD, I would lose interest, so we decided to leave it in until it matured, which wasn't much longer.

I was thirty-four when I bought a four-bedroom home on May 31, 1974. The house had *my* name on it as the owner! First time. The real estate agent and my mom put up some down payment money until I could cash in the CD. The owners didn't charge me the down payment until the CD matured. How often do you hear of that happening? They all trusted that I would pay them when the CD matured. I'm sure there was paperwork to protect all of them. That got us on the road to homeownership, and we have had a home ever since. I shudder to think what could have happened if we didn't have that land.

It was interesting that people seemed to trust me without question. Perhaps having four children and struggling as we did helped them realize we were trustworthy. It was very comforting when someone would say, "That's okay, I trust you." It happened quite often when we first came to Tucson and was a blessing in many cases.

We now have a beautiful home and can see the mountains from our back window and the beautiful Tucson sunsets, but it all started with those twenty-four acres from the divorce. While I should have received much more in the divorce, it did what it needed to do—it got us into a home and off renting.

My youngest son was old enough to attend school when we moved into the new home. The school was considered a "consolidated" school to bring a better ethnicity to the school district. Part of the curriculum was that the children could decide their own goals and decisions. These decisions covered what they studied, when they studied, and when they were to submit their assignments. My son was a good student; however, he would do his assignments and not turn them in. I would attend teachers' conferences, which listed this as their primary problem. My son couldn't explain why he didn't turn in his assignments.

When it was time to leave for school, he didn't want to go, and he wouldn't tell me why. He was six when he went to this school, and as he walked there—it was close to home, the older boys would take his lunch money away. I didn't know this, and he wouldn't tell me. Finally, I followed him to see what was happening and saw the older boys take his money. I went to them and said I had better not hear that they had done it again. We had no further problems. Moms can be fierce beings when necessary!

One of the assignments at the school was to watch the miniseries *Roots*, produced in 1977. I believed the assignment was inappropriate for a six-year-old and asked that he be given a different project in its place. They did. Perhaps that is how parents today should handle situations they don't believe are appropriate for their children. Talk with the teacher about their child only—not speak for all the parents.

I didn't particularly appreciate how the school was operated and looked for another "consolidated" school. The consolidated schools were the only ones kids could attend outside their regular school, and I needed that for my son. There was one that I could drop him off on my way to work. That school wasn't much better because they harassed my son at recess. He was a White child in a minority school, which is what "consolidated" meant. He spent that year at this school, and I moved him again. He was still young enough that it didn't bother him.

By then, the regular school programs were moving away from the consolidated idea, and I put my son in the traditional system. He thrived from then on.

While in this first home, we had a female dog that got pregnant and had puppies while I was at work. My youngest son was older and at home alone. He had never been around when an animal had babies and had no idea what to do. I got a call at work, "Momma, Momma!" As I couldn't leave work, I called my youngest daughter, who went home to help. She had been on the farm and seen animals give birth. They had to give mouth-to-mouth to a couple of the pups to keep them alive. When I got home, both kids were so proud of their accomplishments. It was so cute, and I was proud of my two "veterinarians."

CHAPTER 12

Bought Second Home, Second Marriage

When I sold that house and bought a different one, it was outside the district where my oldest kids went to school. The two oldest went to high school then and didn't want to change schools. They were upset with me for buying the house. I told them that's where I could afford a home—it was in my price range! I went to see the school staff to try and "fix" the problem. School staff told me there was a way for the kids to continue attending Rincon High School. Because of the trauma of the divorce, they could get special permission. Our pastor helped us get the special approval.

My oldest son didn't want to take the bus, so he bought a skateboard, went to school each morning, and came home each evening on the skateboard. It was approximately five and a half miles from our home on Brooks Drive to Rincon High School. He did this for about two years until he got a car and drove to school at sixteen. He was a very determined young man!

My youngest son was always able to convince me to do anything. I don't know why, probably because he was the youngest. If I went home from work with a sick migraine headache, he would talk me into going to find a car "because we needed to get a different one"—or something else ridiculous! That was true. We did need a different vehicle, but not on a day I had a migraine. I was usually so ill that I was throwing up, but we needed to find a car!

When he was about five, I was dating a man who had bought a "ranch." He took my son and me out to go swimming. On the way out, the boyfriend said, "By the way, I discovered that the ranch is a nudist colony."

I was thinking, *Okay, I hope they all stay indoors!* He takes us to the swimming pool, and there are about eight people at the pool. My boyfriend takes off to fix something on the property, leaving my son and me there.

My son says, "Mom, why don't the people have swimming suits on?"

And I casually say, "Because they can't afford them." Now, what was I supposed to say? My older kids thought that was an excellent response at the spur of the moment. It was funny that the people were embarrassed and soon left. We had the pool to ourselves. It was not very smart, though, because neither of us could swim. My son had floaters on his arms. I also had them—yes, a thirty-five-year-old woman with floaters. I felt safe!

I remarried about five years after the divorce. My new husband had four children, two boys and two girls, who lived with their mom in Texas. We would go to Texas to pick them up for the summer months. All but the youngest girl was old enough to tell me I was "not their mother," and getting everyone to work together was not fun. My husband and I had to work during the day, so eight kids old enough to be alone were at home but didn't get along well. I would get a call at work from one of my kids, and my kids would be at one end of the street and his at the other end. So I'd say everyone goes home and stays away from each other until we get home.

I had repeatedly told his kids to stay off the roof, but they thought it was a yard extension. One night, we were leaving to go out to eat, and I needed to shower and get ready. They were on the roof, pushed the ladder off it, and broke the water pipe. Water was everywhere when their dad came home, and he shut it off. When I came home, there was no water for a shower. So I gave my usual speech:

"I am going to my sisters' for a shower and will be back in an hour. The water better be back on!" Luckily, my husband could fix things.

My husband was like a big kid, and while I was at work one day, he took the kids to the animal shelter. They all picked out what they said was a "special pet." This dog could talk, they told me. I get home from work, and all of them are lined up on the sofa—my husband and kids—with big smiles waiting to show me this particular dog and put him through his tricks. I love pets, but the part about who will take care of them is the part that is always on my mind. Everyone said they would. They did, and we had a talking dog added to the household.

Shortly after I got married, our refrigerator broke down, and I went to buy a new one. The store wouldn't sell me a refrigerator without my husband's signature. I argued that I had paid the bills for several years without a man cosigning, and I could pay for a fridge myself. They still refused. I didn't want to purchase a large appliance and put my new husband's name on the bill. So I said, "Fine, I will go somewhere else who will sell *me* a refrigerator." And I did just that. After being bossed around for thirteen years, I finally found a voice!

Learning a lesson from my ex and only being allowed to get low-cost appliances, I would save up to buy what I wanted and get any "bells and whistles" after the divorce. If I couldn't afford it, I waited until I could. And I taught the kids to do the same thing. I drilled into them, "Don't get something cheap that you don't want just to get something. Wait until you can afford what you want." I bought the fridge that I wanted with any extras I wanted! No one told me I couldn't. To this day, I ask the kids, "What do you do when you can't afford it?"

They reply, "Wait until you can and always get what you want!"

It was close to 5:00 p.m. when I was to leave work, and one of the kids called me. One of the eight kids threw a ball, breaking our big double window in the family room. Mom was supposed to take care of this from work with the dad at home! Uh, I don't think so. I suggested that he might want to get someone out there asap to close the window before nightfall. The window was finally fixed, with no one taking the blame.

I never intended to marry to help raise my children, as I believed that was my job. But I did need companionship. It took five years into the new marriage to realize that it wasn't happening, and I had taken on even more responsibility by getting married. We parted amicably and went on with our lives. My goal was "never again!"

During my youngest son's younger years, I went to the Big Brother Group to see if he could get someone that would act as a brother figure in his life. My son's brother was twelve years older and had left home by then. Big Brother managed to find an amicable young man who took a real liking to my son. They did things together weekly, and he stepped in for my son when my boyfriend tried to take over, telling him what he could and couldn't do. I tried not to allow that, but he did it when I didn't know. It was embarrassing for me when the group got involved, but it was what my son needed.

One day, the big brother came to me and said he was going to California and wanted my son to go with him. Oh Wow! My son was my baby. Because he didn't have a father figure, he was a mama's boy and was afraid to do things independently. So I didn't think he would go. I left the decision up to my son. He said he wanted to go. Now I have to make a big decision. Was I going to allow a teenage boy to take off with my son on a trip to California? I finally said he could but cautioned the big brother that he might have to bring my son home early if he got homesick. He said, "Okay," and off they went. Mom was a mess! He finally came home happy, and the trip had done him much good. I wished I had gotten a big brother for his older brother.

My youngest son asked me one day if he was "planned." I just looked at him and didn't know what to say. It was challenging to "plan" a child in those days. I used about every method available and still managed to get pregnant. My husband, at the time, took no responsibility for birth control. So it was an amusing idea for me to plan to have another baby. I don't think I answered him because he and I got flustered. We dropped the question. When he got much older, we finished the conversation.

Once, he took his dirt bike to where all the kids ran their bikes. He was supposed to be home at a particular time, and he wasn't. Of course, I didn't know where this place was because the kids all called it a vulgar name and hadn't told me where it was. It was dark, and he still wasn't home, so I drove around and tried to find him. He finally showed up and said his bike broke down, and he had to push it home. Being a typical mom, I came unglued, first yelling, "Why didn't you stop at a house and call, et cetera?" And then I was so happy that he was okay that I started hugging him. Don't all moms act that way? We get so afraid that we yell when the kid comes home all right, but we are so glad they are okay. I guess the kids will never understand until they have kids of their own.

Yet another time, I had given him a lecture that he should be home from his girlfriend's by 10 p.m. The next night, he wasn't! When he finally got home, I was furious. He said, "Mom, now don't get mad at me. Just listen first." He said he came around a bend on his way home at the proper time; a man was lying on the road. He used my car to stop traffic, walked to the restaurant to get help, stayed until support came, and then came home late. Of course, I was very proud of him and told him so. My kids were "usually" mature in their actions! Did you notice he used my car to stop traffic?

Eventually, he told me he didn't want to go to the school parties anymore. When I asked why, he said he was sick of turning the kids over when they got so drunk to make sure they didn't choke when they threw up. That made me feel good about him but not good about the school parties. Parents left their kids to have parties without chaperoning. Not good! I was glad my son had better sense.

The boys grew out of their clothes faster than the girls, and my youngest son outgrew his shoes the fastest. We were in one of the shoe stores where prices were better, trying on shoes for my youngest son, when my youngest daughter said to me, "Mommy, can I get some new shoes too?"

I looked at her and said, "Honey, do you need new shoes?" And she said that hers had a hole in the bottom. I could have cried. To think that my child was going to school with holes in her shoes because she thought we couldn't afford a new pair for her was heart-breaking. She got new shoes that day, too!

The kids made sure their mom enjoyed all the experiences other moms went through. For instance, we woke up one morning to find many toilet paper rolls among our trees. That was my first and only experience with T-P'ing. I have no idea how the kids got it out of the trees.

You have probably noticed that my youngest son had all the "fun" experiences at home. That's probably because the rest had already left to start their lives.

One day, while I was at work, the kids called me. A man was walking down the street with a pony and cowboy clothes to take pictures of the children. Of course, there was a charge, and the kids wanted to know if the youngest could have his photo taken on the pony. I permitted him to do so, and the man took the pictures and developed them. He then returned, gave us the image, and collected his money. The photos were adorable.

My youngest son could not keep track of his keys to the house. We replaced the house key so often that I was afraid half the neighborhood had a set of keys to our home. Finally, my son would leave his bedroom window open just a crack. He could always get in the house and didn't have to tell me that he had lost the key again!

One day, I found the window open and asked why. The jig was up. Now, I knew his secret. It came in handy when Mom needed to get in one day and couldn't. Can't you see me crawling through his bedroom window and sliding down to the floor over the chair? I'm sure it wasn't very graceful. I have *never* been considered "graceful."

Yet another day, my younger son went outside to the backyard and came running back, yelling, "Mom, there is a bike in our backyard."

I thought, *Okay, now what is going on?* We went back outside, and sure enough, there was an expensive bike in our backyard. I called the police, and they came to check it out. They made a case file and told my son that the bicycle was his if no one claimed it within a particular time. They took the bike with them. Well, that sounded pretty good to my son, and he would call the police station often to see if anyone claimed the bicycle.

No one claimed the bicycle when the time was up, and the police called us to come down and pick it up. My son was so excited because it was an expensive bike, and now it was his. When we got to the police station, the officer checked the lost and found department, but they couldn't find the bike. It was nowhere. They never did find the bike. My son wanted to know how this could be. No one claimed the bicycle, and no one could find the bike—now try explaining that to your kid. He was so disappointed, and there was nothing I could do to fix it—an unfortunate experience for him and me.

The kids always felt comfortable offering our home to their friends if they needed a safe place. I never knew how many kids would be in the house when I woke up. Many times, there were more than four. My kid who offered a haven to their friend said the kid and their parents were fighting at home. It never posed a problem for us. They never stayed more than a day. By that time, the family had settled their differences. I was proud that they felt comfortable offering our home. I was glad it was never my kid that had to stay at someone else's house because we were fighting. The kids and their families that stayed over believed they were safe at our house. That's always good to know.

Just as I always was working, the kids started working as soon as they were old enough, and they all held jobs at fast-food places. My daughter came home from work one night, went into the house, and told me that she heard a loud noise as she went around the corner to our street. We went outside and checked her car; the left-back window was broken. The projectile went from the left-back window through the right-front window. She would have been dead if it had gone straight from the left. We called the police and reported it. The next day, she got the window fixed. They never found anyone who had shot a gun in the area.

Two weeks later, someone smashed her car into the car in front of her. She called me and said, "But, Mom, the front window didn't get broken." She thought that was exceptional. My doctor couldn't understand why I didn't have white hair!

When my oldest son was working and cleaning up after work late at night, they went outside, and the door shut behind them. My son called to see if I could come and get them. Somehow, they would be able to get back in, finish cleaning up, and then I could take him home. That was so funny. We mention it and get a laugh out of everyone to this day. When they discovered they were locked out, the expressions on their faces must have been priceless.

It seemed like I was always looking for ways to earn extra money. Staff from the computer department at the police department became friends with me and knew I was interested in computers. They said I should take some classes. Computers sounded very difficult, and I told them that. I didn't think there was any way that I could accomplish working on a computer. They said they were just like puzzles, and they would help me. So I took a class at Pima Community College and liked it. I asked my friends in the computer department what the best computer was, and they suggested the KayPro computer. It was supposed to have all the memory you would ever need. What a laugh that was! They never realized in a few years that those computers would have gigabytes!

Anyway, I took several classes and learned to program computers. The KayPro had programs for word processing and a database, which I also studied. With my database knowledge, I offered to enter information into the computer for others so that they could print labels for their customers. I got an order to enter data for a client who gave me $10,000 to enter and proof the information. It seemed I was in the right place at the right time for these extra jobs. They helped keep us going financially.

While getting ready for work one day, the high school called to verify that my youngest son had been out of school due to illness; I said he had been ill and hung up. The school called two more times. When I got home from work, I asked my son what was going on as I was late for work. He said, "Oh, they thought my girlfriend was answering, and I told them I just have a very young mother." I guess after the third time with the same answer and the same person, they believed him. Being a young mother, the kids had problems because I was so young.

My youngest son also gets very dark in the summer, and the staff at the school thought he was Mexican, so they put him in special classes. People called him after school at night, asked questions about his studies, and tried to help him. "What is going on?" I asked my son. He said he was in a particular program to help him advance. My son was smart and didn't need extra help; however, they thought he did.

Once a year, all the sponsors from the program came to talk to the kids. Years later, he told me that one time they were going around the room, asking the kids about their ethnicity. When they got to my son, he said he was Irish and German. They all stopped in their tracks. They couldn't believe their ears. They asked a few more questions and were convinced of what he said, so they immediately said he wasn't qualified for the program and kicked him out of the room. I just found this out after thirty-one years. It is amazing what you find out about your kids years later!

Trips to Mexico were the going thing for kids, and my youngest son was no different. However, he and his friends thought they were invincible. They took off for Mexico one year in an old car with four bad tires. I didn't know this! They had to replace five tires before they got back. How could they replace five, you ask? So did we! They were getting old tires from the shops in Mexico, and one was so bad that it also went flat. Yes, they replaced five tires on one trip. We laughed about that one, also.

When my younger son was still in high school, he came home excited with a car he had bought. He came rushing up to the door and wanted me to come out and see it. I could see an older car from the porch, a 1936 Plymouth that needed a paint job and lots of work. Little did I know how much work there was until I got to the street to see the inside. There were no floorboards. I asked him how he got it home and where he had put his feet. He laughed and said, "On the struts." Only my kids!

Little did I know that he would have to take me to the doctor in that car when I had a bad migraine and couldn't drive myself. He said he felt so bad because I was sick and there was no place for my feet to get comfortable. Good thing I don't remember it.

That car created more excitement in the family for years to come. At Christmas, he wanted "purple" paint so he and his friends could paint it. The color was costly, and it took the whole family to buy what he needed. When the time came to paint the car, all the friends but one pooped out, and my son and the remaining friend painted the car purple. It was purple until the day he sold it, many years later. And it had run by then. We called it his purple people eater!

He also got another car and took it apart in the driveway. It was an old Volkswagen. He and his friend had the engine in the driveway and were working away. I saw that the engine was in the back, where the trunk and gas tank usually are and asked where the gas tank and trunk were. He said, "Oh, the gas tank is in the front." Just what a mom wants to hear—in front of where her kid sits in case of an accident!

The following words that came out of my mouth were "Get rid of it!" He said I said it with such authority that he knew there was no room for discussion.

When he told me this years later, I asked him what he did, and he said, "I got rid of it!" Wow, I didn't know that could happen so quickly. I don't remember it! Sometimes you forget things to protect yourself!

My oldest son came home with a motorcycle one day. He was old enough that I couldn't use the famous "you can't because Mom says you can't." He thought he was cute by asking if I would like a ride, thinking there was no way his mom would ride a motorcycle. He didn't know, but I had ridden a bike before. I had carried him in my arms when he was a baby, and his dad drove us down to his grandparents, who were going to watch him while we rode the motorcycle.

So casually, I said sure and got on the back of his bike. The look on his face was priceless. We went around the block, and he had to remind me to lean to the left or right side so we didn't tip over. It is always fun when you can surprise your kids.

Sometimes I just wanted the kids to realize life is to be enjoyed and not taken too seriously, so I would say funny things. The refrigerator stopped making ice cubes several times, and the last time I said, "I bought an ice cube maker to embarrass the refrigerator into making ice cubes." Guess what? It makes ice cubes periodically, whereas before, it didn't.

The kids and grandkids thought, *Mom (Grandma Sandy) is silly.* That is good. We need to laugh more often.

These silly sayings kept my kids on their toes. They never knew what would come out of their mom's mouth. I would say something stupid, and they would laugh at me. Sometimes I said something "stupid" and didn't realize it was ridiculous! It also was a calming technique for all of us. Sometimes my mom and I would have to ask the Lord to put his hand over our mouths because we had a hard time not saying something wrong. That was a "biggie" for Mom and me.

The kids excelled in school and were in the band and other after-school events. My oldest son played the trumpet and several other instruments. He was in the "Mood Jazz Band" at Rincon High School. It was great to see how their trumpets turned side to side in rhythm with the music. I was so proud of him. My oldest daughter played the flute. When she was young, she could remember the music from school. We bought her a little piano for Christmas, and she could play the songs "by ear" like her grandma Rose. My youngest daughter played the clarinet, was in the first chair, and could play several instruments. My youngest son played the clarinet. He didn't play for long because he wanted to be in sports. He was in wrestling and football and probably didn't have the time to practice as much as the other three did. Most of them could play several instruments. I made sure they had music lessons if they wanted because I never could and always wanted to learn to play a musical instrument.

I have tried three times to teach myself to play the piano or organ, and each time I gave up after several weeks. I couldn't get the count down, and my fingers were short, so I could not reach the full essential spread of the keys. I decided it just wasn't "going to happen."

Kids in the band were required to march during the rodeo parade in Tucson, which was the longest nonmotorized parade. They had to have their shoes freshly cleaned. Of course, at the end of the procession, they might have stepped in many piles of horse manure, but they were clean when they started. I remember the kids taking great care to have immaculate shoes and uniforms. The parade went through downtown Tucson in those days. I could take my lunch hour and watch the kids march. They enjoyed being in the parade with the band.

Whenever there was a function that the kids were in, such as a parade, a band concert, or a wrestling match (for my youngest son), we didn't have money for anything fancy afterward as a reward. But they could always count on going out for an ice cream cone later and looked forward to it. Ice cream is an integral part of our lives as it was when I was a child!

When my youngest son was wrestling, I watched him, and it was tough for me to sit still when he was sat on or got thrown. I told him once that I almost got up, went out there, and threw the kid off him. He thought I was serious and wasn't a happy camper. "Mom, don't ever do that, please," he said. Of course, I wouldn't, but it was hard to watch if your kid was getting beaten up.

As a young mother, I tried to teach my kids to be honest and trustworthy. Working at the police department was a great motivator. One of the kids came out of a store with a toy. I knew I had not paid for it and was upset, thinking someone would stop us as shoplifters. That would not have been good for an employee of the police department! Can't you just see the headlines in the newspaper, "Police employee arrested for shoplifting!" We went back into the store, and I made my son explain that they had not paid for it. The clerk understood that Mom was making a point and spoke with my son. We paid for it and left with Mom, explaining what a bad choice he had made.

On another day, my youngest son and I were at a grocery store, standing in front of the cashier's stand. On the floor was a one-dollar bill. Trying to teach my son a good lesson, I picked up the dollar bill, handed it to the cashier, and said it was on the floor. I hoped that whoever lost it would come and claim it. Remember, I was always broke. At any rate, as we left the store, my son said, "You know, Mom, that lady probably just put the dollar in her pocket!" Was it a teachable moment or not?

We couldn't afford much entertainment, so we did everything we could that was free and that the kids would enjoy. Hands Across America was one of the functions we attended on Sunday, May 25, 1986. Only the youngest two kids were still at home, and we had to drive to a place set out for the event in our area. It was an attempt to have people across the United States hold hands for fifteen minutes, from Los Angeles to New York City. The media estimated that five to six million people participated, and my kids were part of it. It was a fascinating event to attend. We all received buttons to signify that we had participated. I asked my daughter recently if she remembered being there, and she said she did. It was a special time for the kids and me to enjoy together. It was free and patriotic. What could have been better?

My oldest daughter was brilliant and on her way to graduating in three years. However, when she was fourteen, she told me she was pregnant. She had regularly dated the same boy from school and wanted to keep the baby. I couldn't see a fourteen-year-old child having a baby and tried to talk her out of it. I know it wasn't my shining moment as a mother. I looked up everything I could read to understand what I was talking about and finally agreed that she was right. I was thirty-six when I became a grandmother. When I told the people at work that I was a grandmother, they said, "Yeah, right." I had to show them a picture of the baby and me to prove I was a grandmother.

Of course, my daughter couldn't continue school and had to drop out. Later she got her GED and got good jobs with her knowledge and skills.

She and her boyfriend got married in the hospital, waiting for the baby to be born! From there, they moved in with his parents. I wasn't allowed to visit because his parents didn't want me at their house.

Eventually, things smoothed over, and I could see the baby. That was because the family fought, and my daughter would call me to come to pick her up. I had to take her back to work with the baby. They stayed in a room for staff until work was over, and I would take her and the baby to my house. The two would make up, she would go home, and it would start again. "Mom, can you come and pick me up?" Of course, I always did. My mom picked her up if I couldn't. They finally got divorced.

Years later, my granddaughter and I talked, and she asked me why I hadn't come to see her when she was a baby. I don't know how she knew, but I told her why, and then she asked about my wanting her mom to get an abortion. I told her that I wouldn't lie to her and that it was true. I told her that at fourteen, I was scared for her mom. She said she had a fourteen-year-old stepsister, and she could understand. I told her we were so happy her mother hadn't done so and that we loved her so much. She accepted my explanation, and we never discussed it again.

My dad could build anything, and my youngest son is much like our dad. He became a welder like my dad. Unfortunately, he never knew my dad, as my dad passed away before he was born.

After graduation, my son wanted to go to school to be an underwater welder—a dangerous job. He talked me into signing for him to go to school and sign for a loan. Supposedly, the loan wasn't going to cost me anything. Right! I have heard that one before. When he got to California and arrived at the school site, he discovered the school was nothing like they had described it to him in high school. His teacher—yes, the teacher at the school—got injured. He told me what had happened and that nothing was as they had told him. He said, "Mom, can I come home?" I thought it was terrific for a youngster to know that they shouldn't just keep plugging ahead and rack up the bills for a program that isn't what it was all cracked up to be. Of course, I said yes immediately and was glad to have him home. The loans were all canceled, and I didn't pay anything. Remarkable! Unbeknownst to me, he had given up a scholarship to go to the school, and they would not honor the scholarship when he came back. That was too bad. The scholarship would have been such a help to him in getting his college tuition paid.

After that experience, as a high school graduate with no scholarship to fall back on, my son talked me into taking my car to Alaska to apply for a job on the fishing boats during the summer. That way, he could make money for college. He and his friend took my two-tone Chevrolet Monte Carlo with swivel front seats. That car was my "everything in a car!" I was so proud of it.

On the way, they had problems in a snow blizzard in Oregon or Washington and were under the hood in shorts and T-shirts with their buts sticking out when the police stopped to see what two teenagers were doing with such a nice car. They had quite a time convincing the police that it was my car. My son always wore shorts in the winter.

The children had all graduated from high school and were married. Their father never took the time to come, send a congratulatory card, or give any gifts. They were nonevents to him. The kids all took it in stride and were not concerned. They were terrific examples of well-adjusted kids. I must have done something right!

Because of events in my life, I was scared to stay alone. My son was my last child to leave home, and I would have been alone while he was in Alaska. I convinced his girlfriend to stay with me until he came back. She was there at night. She was a sweetheart and a comfort to me.

He and his friend got the job and left for Alaska. He would write as often as possible and explain what they were doing. He said he volunteered to do the yucky stuff first, and then he would have better days later. They knew he would be willing to do those distasteful jobs and relied on him. The boat was a rickety old boat. He sent me a picture of it; by the looks of it, it was not seaworthy! He said one of the young men saw the conditions were so bad when they got to Alaska that he started crying—it was that bad.

They discovered that the boat may need to go into Russian territory and that my son needed a passport in case that happened. Getting a passport usually takes weeks or months. The company must have had connections because they got the visa quickly. But he did get the passport just in case they went into Russian waters. They never ventured into Russian territory!

They were paid all at once when they got off the boat. The guys would play cards in their off-hours, and losses went against their paychecks. My son said some of the guys had no money left when they got home. They lost it all playing cards! I hope they learned a lesson if they went back the following year.

CHAPTER 13

Police Department

During the turmoil of everyday life, my ex was getting remarried. His fiancé was Catholic and wanted to get married in the Catholic Church. The problem was that my ex was divorced. The solution they came up with was to annul our marriage. To them, that sounded reasonable. That was ridiculous as we had four children and had been married for thirteen years. I sputtered to my mom, sister, brother, and anyone else who would listen.

Eventually, I got a letter from a priest asking me to set up a meeting to discuss this annulment. The letter, dated June 30, 1975, blamed me for the marriage not working out. It said, "At the time of the marriage, Sandra was seventeen, and her ex [I am not disclosing his name] was twenty. There was a premarital pregnancy; the parents objected to the marriage. Sandra had moved to Arizona, and her father offered [her ex] a job in Arizona in view of her longing to maintain her relationship with [her ex]! The preliminary investigation forms point to an unstable union and much immaturity."

He blamed me for the divorce and said my parents objected, which was not true. My parents were very supportive of us as they knew how much I cared for him. He was the reason for the divorce, nothing else. His abuse became too much, which was the reason for the divorce.

We set a date with the priest, and my mom took me to the appointment. She sat in the outer lobby while I talked (shouted) with the priest. He couldn't see a problem; I saw all kinds of issues. *He told me that I could cooperate, or they could do it without me.* (Control by the priest!) After thirteen years of marriage and four children, I explained that it was wrong. How can you annul such a marriage? I asked him what I was supposed to tell my children. He said I shouldn't tell them! He said the church had no problem with this arrangement. Mom said she heard me shouting in the lobby. I was distraught with the discussion!

The priest had not settled anything but had gotten me more upset. I never found out what happened. I understand you have to pay for this privilege, which is not cheap.

My first job upon arriving in Tucson was working at the University of Arizona. It was supposed to be a big plus because your children could go to the university free of charge, I believe, when they graduated high school; however, the wages were meager. With four children to raise and child support of fifty dollars per child, that wasn't enough to get a decent apartment, food, clothing, electricity, et cetera. People tried to tell me it was worth it to continue working at the university if the kids could get a college education without cost. But I told them I had to get them to college-age first!

My boss understood and told me to go to the human resources office and see if there were any openings for a better job as I had the skills for a better job. He also realized that I was working at a higher classification than I was getting paid. The people in Human Resources were distraught with me for coming in and asked if my boss knew I was there. I told them that he had sent me! Nothing came of it, so I looked elsewhere and found a job at the Tucson police department. My brother was a police officer there, but I didn't want people to think I used him to get in, so I went and applied without telling anyone.

We had to take a typing test. It was on one of the old portable typewriters. Everyone was typing as fast as they could to get a big score. I plugged along to get fewer errors. After we took the test, they told us they took ten points off for every mistake we made. The women almost fainted. My slow as a turtle came out first! My score was number one, and my interview got me into the police department. Then I told the family, and my brother couldn't believe it.

I had the job; however, I had to lose weight to keep it. There was a weight minimum to work at the police department. It was tough to lose weight because I have had a thyroid issue since childhood. I was finally able to meet the requirement when my probation was up. I loved that job and worked there for two years before moving to another city department.

The police department was my first successful money-paying job upon arriving in Tucson. It was so exciting working for the police. I thought they were real heroes, and my brother was one of them. You couldn't have it any better. This time frame was right after my divorce, and I was nervous. I would get terrible migraine headaches, get sick, and throw up. I also was very depressed. I was losing weight like crazy because I was so depressed. I lost more weight after losing the required weight to keep the job. Incredible timing, right?

Again, my sister saw what was happening and called my mom, who immediately decided to take me to the doctor. The doctor gave me some pill that must have been super strong because I snapped out of it fast. I told Mom and my sister that they should let me lose a bit more weight next time before taking me to the doctor. I had a weight problem and always will!

At work, the people cared for me and made me feel okay. My supervisor sent me home using her sick leave more than once. I will never forget her empathy and generosity.

While working at the police department, my oldest son called me one afternoon and said a group of kids had beaten him and his girlfriend up on their way home from school. The records department where I worked was on the second floor, and the police officers were on the first floor. I didn't even take the time to call. I ran down the stairs to tell them what happened and asked them to go and check on the kids.

They drove the kids around the block to see if they could identify those who beat them up. They could only recognize one because our kids covered their heads, trying not to get hurt. They arrested only that one. The group of kids had been going from one school to another, causing problems. Come to find out, the person they identified was one of several who had beaten a man and set him on fire on A Mountain called Sentinal Peak in Tucson. The man died. It was a big story at the time. Working at the police department, I was able to read the report. It was scary to read and then realize these kids had hurt our kids. It could have been so much worse for our kids.

Our children went to court once, but then they stopped our kids' trial because of the more significant legal suit of the murdered man. While our kids were at the hearing, the arrested kids gave them so much trouble that the judge put our kids in his office to keep them safe. My son said they followed him into the restroom and threatened him.

Our kids had to go to the doctor after being beaten up. My son had stitches, and his girlfriend had to go to the chiropractor because her back was out. We didn't get any reimbursement because the trial stopped, and the parents had no money anyway.

During the early 1970s, there was a gas shortage. People had to wait in line; sometimes, the gas ran out before they got to the pumps. As an employee of the police department, I was a "crucial employee." I had the unique privilege of always being able to purchase gas. Some people were not so lucky. We had to buy locks for our gas tank, or people would siphon the gas from the tank. It was a nerve-racking time to be working, and I was grateful to be able to purchase gas when needed.

We worked three shifts at the police department, which was difficult for most women. I usually asked for the rotating shift, allowing me to pay less for childcare. The rotating shifts were two to ten, ten to six, and six to two. It was not a sought-after shift because you couldn't get proper sleep. They usually could accommodate my request because no one else wanted to work rotating shifts.

Whenever we had items we no longer needed, we always gave them to the Gospel Rescue Mission in Tucson. They don't charge for their items and are very generous. When I heard of a woman who needed help desperately and was depressed, I took her to the Gospel Rescue Mission. They asked her what she needed. They filled my car with a giant turkey (it was near Thanksgiving) and a bag of potatoes, and my trunk with food. Then they asked her if she needed any furniture. Yes, they are a fantastic nonprofit group. The woman sat in my car and cried.

I had asked our church for help when the woman needed it, and they said they could give her a "bag" of groceries. The church gave most of the items to groups outside Tucson. That didn't sit well with me. The church never understood that a single mom with four young children could use help, and they didn't want to ask for it. During a meeting, I explained that the church people should know that and not expect the mom to ask. The pastor looked at me and said, "Sandy, you are right." That is why I took her to the Gospel Rescue Mission. They were much more generous, and there was no charge for the items.

When you donate items to Good Will, people must pay for them. Being a single mom with little income, I wanted others to be able to get things for free.

CHAPTER 14

City Clerk's Department

One of the larger departments in the City of Tucson consistently had openings. The women in the police department had the skills to fill the positions, and many of us applied for the jobs and were hired. The pay was also more significant, and there was a greater chance for advancement. That was a promising advancement in our career path. The police department didn't have as many advancement opportunities. They also couldn't afford to lose qualified people. They finally had to limit how long we had to wait before we could go to the new job.

Unfortunately, that happened when a major department hired one of my friends and me. We had to wait a couple of months before we could go over. It was worth it, though, because I gradually advanced from the Elections Clerk to an Administrative Assistant III and was second-in-command in my division by the time I retired. While working there, I was assigned some excellent projects, such as recodifying the City of Tucson Charter and Code, running the city's early voting section for elections, and many other exciting projects.

Mental abuse or harassment doesn't necessarily happen only in relationships. It often occurs in the workplace. What is it like in the workplace? You will see as you continue to read.

The department I moved to consisted of the overall department head and three divisions with an assistant department head. During my time there, I worked for each of the three assistant department heads.

When I first transferred to the new department, I met many women who had initially worked in the police department. One I particularly liked because she was friendly and helpful. She was an absolute sweetheart. As my time working there continued, this woman became friends with one of the executives, and her attitude changed. She eventually married the man. She now became interested in getting ahead. The two worked together to advance her to the top of the department. She became the department head when he retired.

She believed she could move her staff wherever she wanted when she got to the top. She moved team members even if they applied for a position, were interviewed, and received the job. She did that to me. That wasn't my belief, but I had nothing to back me up when she moved me around at will. Later, you will read that moving me around was done to place another woman in line for my position. The staff made changes to my job to accomplish their goal.

Shortly after I transferred to the new department, the department head talked to me about something I believed wasn't correct. Naive me, I told the top man I thought he was wrong! He looked at me, shook his head, and agreed with me. Through that action, he felt that I was trainable as a good employee and was hard on me in a good way. He explained if I had used the wrong word in a memo and why it was wrong. He gave me challenging projects and expected me to do a good job. After many years, he retired, and I thanked him and told him that he was hard on me, but I had learned a lot from him.

One assignment was to review the file on the mayors of the city of Tucson and identify corrections, if necessary. The list showed the name of the mayor and their service date. The first mayor on the list became an "issue." He was not the mayor of Tucson because Tucson was not a city at the time. He was a commissioner of the territory. I continued with the list and found that some of the term dates were incorrect. On several occasions, staff entered their appointment length using the date elected instead of appointment dates. Terms begin on the day the mayor and council swear in the person. The election date is only the date the person was elected.

I turned in the report, suggesting several changes. I don't know if that happened. I was not in a "need to know" position, and someone else was assigned to continue the project—or not.

I believed it was necessary to tell my immediate boss that I was looking for a better-paying job because I wasn't getting child support regularly. I thought that a reasonable employee didn't surprise their boss in those days by leaving without notice. Now it is different. Recently I read that you shouldn't tell your boss you are looking for another position. Times sure do change. After my experience, I can see why times have changed.

At any rate, my boss talked with me and thought he had convinced me not to look for another job until the election was over. I wasn't getting child support on time and had problems feeding my four children. So it was necessary to look for a higher-paying job. He felt people should live within their means and said so to others. He believed I was trying to get a raise. It is easy to say such things if you make a big salary.

When I didn't stop looking, he called the office and told staff to move me before returning from his appointment. He called again to see if it had happened. The team said they hadn't moved me, and he told them to move me immediately. Upon his direction, the staff moved me to a different section. I retained my old duties and now had additional responsibilities. My new tasks included typing meeting notes, but I was hard of hearing. I didn't tell my supervisor that I was hard of hearing because I was embarrassed. As a result of the hearing problem, I could not distinguish which person was speaking on the tape. At the same time, I continued with my other duties. Now I was basically working two jobs.

My evaluation became due, and I didn't receive it. I asked my new boss why. He said it "would be okay when I got it."

I asked him what that meant. I learned she gave me a low evaluation because I couldn't type the necessary number of pages. I had never received a bad evaluation. He changed the review to include *all* the duties I was performing and gave me an acceptable score.

None of this would have happened had I obeyed my boss and stopped looking for another job. When a boss threatens you, it is harassment in the workplace.

I was mentally harassed many more times, usually by this man and his wife. You will be able to recognize the manipulation of my duties to make my life miserable, and I believe they hoped I would quit. Thankfully, I had a few people looking out for me. To this day, I have nightmares about this job.

While working at the city clerk's office, the City Water Department staff put another person's bill with an identical name to mine on my bill. The other person's bill was delinquent. They were getting paid for the late bill by putting the amount on my account, believing we were the same person. However, that was not true. We were two different people, and the Water Department staff did not check that out before moving the bill to my account. In trying to correct the error, the burden of proving the error fell on my shoulders. I had to bring in documents to prove the person was not me. The person in question lived in Alaska. Only then did they remove the erroneous charges from my account.

My goal always is to help bring other women up with me when I am in a position to do so. Oddly, that is not how many other women see it. I have seen it happen so often. It happened all the time in our office. The women bring the men up with them but hold the women back. Women who succeed should show other women how to achieve and help them up the ladder. I have always tried to do that. I only wish other women would feel the same. When you have made it, help other women also get ahead. We need to take care of each other.

Coworkers are uncomfortable when an employee gives a complete 100 percent on the job. My parents taught us to perform our work at 100 percent, and I usually gave 110 percent. When you are smart, a good worker, and honest, that doesn't make you a friend of others. I believe coworkers feel threatened by a dedicated employee who puts in a full day's work. Two people—one I *knew* didn't like me, and I knew what to expect from her after a while.

I thought the other person was a friend until my "real friends" told me what she said about me behind my back. She knew the Pima County Elections staff and told them I made the other people work while taking life easy. That was the job I went to on vacation and depended on for extra income. I now knew that this person was not my friend as nothing could be farther from the truth. But it was to the county's advantage salary-wise to replace me. They replaced me with the person that I had been training. In my eyes, she was not ready yet. She made significant mistakes that I had to correct while teaching her. The year she took over the job, the people under her came to my office and said, "She will have us put in jail. She is not following the State code and charter for elections." They were worried, but there was nothing I could do. She continued on the job, and nothing happened to bring attention to any errors. I guess everyone was happy with her performance.

Something else I learned was very disturbing. One of my bosses told me that I shouldn't be so trusting of a particular person. I had thought this person was my friend. Later I learned differently. If a boss you trust tells you to be careful of someone, listen to them. They are in "the know" of the department.

My drive, knowledge, and opportunity gave me many ways to increase my worth in the office. Following are some examples, and I hope they interest you and do not bore you. Perhaps the ideas will give you some ideas to improve your job.

I applied for an open position as a computer representative for the department. It was an excellent opportunity as I loved computers, and the new position was a career advancement. I was accepted for the job and began to computerize several office areas. One of the tasks I computerized was the information from incoming mail and items from the mayor's and council's meetings. Previously, the information was typed onto index cards and filed. To add the new information, you had to find the card, type it on the card, and refile the card. With the computerized program, staff entered meeting information and incoming mail into the computer. It could perform a search to find the information quickly when the public or other departments requested it. We still had the old data on the index cards because we didn't have staff to input the old data into the computers, but the new information was more accessible and faster.

In another office section, the staff compiled the governmental agenda materials for the weekly governmental meetings and processed the approved paperwork. Among the documents were intergovernmental agreements (IGAs) between the city of Tucson and other governmental agencies. My division head was over this area, and the IGAs had a backlog for months and even years. That meant the agreements could not be implemented until all the governments signed. I began closing the backlog by writing letters with copies of the documents to each jurisdiction. When I moved to another area, the backlog was much shorter.

An opening came up for an administrator over the records division. I applied and received the promotion. It was exciting because I saw many things that needed modernizing. After working in the area for a while and seeing how the department worked, it was time to upgrade the system gradually. It is challenging for staff and administration to make changes. Be sure you don't start making changes before understanding why the current system is in place.

There had not been an administrator in this area, and I instinctively knew the supervisor was having a problem with me becoming her boss. Previously, she didn't report to anyone. So I tried to make the transition easy for everyone. I would greet everyone in the morning as I came to work, but no one greeted me. That was surprising as everyone knew me, and I thought they liked me. Finally, one of the brave women told me their boss, the woman I *knew* didn't like me, had told them *not* to acknowledge me. She didn't want them interacting with me. She didn't want them to trust me. That never faded, but some women could see that I meant well. Those who trusted me and took my advice advanced like the one who went with me later to work on the elections.

Problem areas fascinated me. If I have to work, I look for problem areas to "fix." I look for projects that can be done better, faster, or less complicated. I'm your girl. The department head knew this and put me in many such problem areas. That's why I enjoyed my job during this period of employment.

An area that no one seemed to think was an issue was that all the public record file cabinets were in and around the staff. The file cabinets were the barriers between the desks. When you received a public record request, you had to run all over the office to find the file cabinet and information in and around the staff. It seemed inefficient and disruptive to staff.

With the computerization of the information completed while I was the information technician, I implemented a color-coding system for the files and computerized the folders.

When I was made administrator of the area, it appeared that the team should have more privacy to work better and that the files should be in one place, not scattered around the room. The staff kept the office machines in the next room for easy access. I started to take measurements to see if the files fit in that room. By creating a diagram of the area and the filing cabinets, I discovered that we could place all the files in the room. It would work if we put them around the walls and made rows down the middle of the room with the office machines.

My immediate boss had no problem with any changes as he had confidence in my plans, but I had to get the okay of the department head. The department head saw the value in putting all the public records in a separate room where we could lock the door and agreed to the change. It was a significant improvement. Upon finalization, I recommended adding partitions to the budget for staff. The sections included a segregated place for my office, where I could have private meetings if necessary.

The staff had separate compartments, and I had a private area to meet with staff for reviews. When I retired, the next administrator took all the partitions down as she believed it wasn't a good idea to have separate compartments for the staff. They weren't too excited about the color-coded system either, so I don't know if they maintained it or not. That is what is so frustrating. When staff updates a plan, new people come in and put in their ideas without reviewing what is already there. That is why I said not to make changes until you understand why the current system is in place. The office was going backward instead of forward. I saw that happen so many times.

As an administrator, you are now in management and can offer suggestions for the budget. That is how I got the partitions for staff. I also checked what it would cost to paint our old desks. We couldn't replace them, but I thought it would make staff happy to have better-looking desks. The price wasn't that high, and it was approved. I put it in for our "division" only as I only had a say in our budget. The other administrators in their division didn't ask for the same thing in their division. When it came time for my staff's desks to be painted, they were done on a Saturday to not interfere with the workday. The budget listed the number of desks to be painted. That became a problem when the department head wanted one more desk painted. The desk was in another division. I had to eliminate one desk—mine—from my division to accommodate his wishes. The painters didn't want that to happen and agreed to paint my desk.

One thing I implemented for all the computers was backing up the files daily using the grandfather-father-son method. This method allows you to have three different versions in case one backup is destroyed. You back up the files on the first day to your grandfather's disk. On the second day, you call the file Father; on the third, the file is Son. On the fourth day, use the grandfather disk. Continue rotating the files in this manner. You will always have the three most recent versions of your work. This method came in very handy while writing this book. More than once, I had to go back to the previous version.

Employees were offered "differential compensation" during one budget cycle. It was something new, and you could put money from the top of your paycheck into a "differed plan" and not pay taxes on it until you took it out many years later when you retired at a lower tax rate. I started with five dollars to see how much it would affect my paycheck as we lived paycheck to paycheck. It wasn't much, so I would put more into the plan each time I got a raise. By the time I retired, there were over sixty thousand dollars in the account. So if you think you can't contribute to a retirement plan, start small and work your way up. But do start.

CHAPTER 15

Holidays, Art Classes, Absentee

When holidays came around, my family rotated celebrating them, so no one person had to do all the baking, planning, and paying for the event. I loved to entertain in those days and do unique things like baking all the hamburger buns for barbecue hamburgers for the family. It took weeks of baking and putting them in the freezer, but we had a giant freezer, and I enjoyed doing it for the family.

On one occasion, we had breakfast midmorning, and we had pancakes, eggs, bacon, waffles, and any other breakfast food imaginable. You could choose what you wanted. It was fun. Another time we had a strawberry shortcake party midafternoon because the kids liked my shortcake made with Bisquick. We had large bowls of strawberries, whipped cream, ice cream, shortcakes, and anything associated with strawberry shortcake. It was indeed a success.

Thanksgiving and Christmas were the same. Lots of goodies. I would start making cookies weeks ahead of time and put them in the freezer. One year, I made twenty-eight different kinds of cookies. There were the kids' specials—cutouts, peanut butter blossoms, ginger cookies, and chocolate chip cookies. They loved the candy I made with cornflakes. Other moms probably made the candy. You just melt milk chocolate and mix in cornflakes. You could add a lot of cornflakes to make lots of candy. Then you put spoons full of the mix on a tray and refrigerate. Oh, were they good! Now it is more challenging to find the blocks of chocolate that were available in those days.

While working downtown in Tucson, I decided to take some art classes at one of the art studios after work. The course was charcoal drawing, and we learned to draw depth into our pictures. One night, the instructor told us that we would be drawing nude models the following week. The men in the class thought that was great. They all made comments that they would be sure to make that class. Come next week for class time; only one man was brave enough to come. The teacher was very professional. We only had a few minutes to draw before the model changed to a different position. The model was female. We also made large self-portraits. I found mine recently, and it is good enough to hang.

After that first class, I started going to art shows and talking with the artists. They told me oil paint is best if you want to become a professional. One of the artists gave me the name of a teacher in art who was very reasonable. I called and set up a time for a class. My mom and I went for a couple of years.

My mom went with me as I was still a scaredy-cat to do anything alone. It was a good time for the two of us to bond. We had a good time, and Mom painted some excellent pictures that she hung on her walls at home. Mine were also good, and they are hanging in our home. When I took on the second job, I had to stop painting for a while and now hope to get back to it after completing the book! They say anyone can paint, so don't be afraid to try. Mom had never drawn in her life and said, "Oh, Sandy, I can't draw." You might surprise yourself and become a budding artist. There are examples of my paintings in the photo section.

As the artists recommended, I used oils. I also chose to use a palette knife. I am very impatient, and it took too long to wash the paintbrushes. You take a paper towel and wipe off the blade of the palette knife. It was much faster! The art teacher gave us "recipes" for mixing the paints for "desert green" and the other vegetation in Tucson. He was an excellent teacher and an outstanding artist. His mom was also an artist, and we saw some of her work. I received one of her paintings as a drawing in a contest. Mom and I took several classes with him. Years later, we found the artist, and I asked if he had written a book. It would have been a bestseller. He said no. Too bad.

When I worked in the city, they hired women working in elections as "clerks" and men as "election technicians" for the Clerk's office. At the time, I realized this was wrong but was not in a position to do anything about it. When I was finally promoted to a supervisory role and needed to hire staff, I suggested to management that this was discrimination. They said men had to lift and do heavy work, so they were technicians. Some women applied for technician jobs and did the lifting to receive higher pay. This argument did not sit well, and when I became an administrator, I argued and won that from then on, the men and women were hired by their work level. They didn't know what they were up against when they initially hired *me*! I stick up for the underdog—I was there long enough to be able to do so.

There became an opening for an assistant city clerk in the elections division. One of the critical requirements was listed as "extensive background information on computers." I wasn't particularly excited about the promotion, but because it involved computer knowledge, I applied. When the promotion was announced, I was at home. The city clerk called to tell me she had chosen a certain man "because she felt she owed it to him." He had *no* computer training! I believed that was a pretty sorry excuse for hiring this person, but because I didn't want the job, I just said, "Okay." That person never did any computer work. It was given to me whenever I was moved into elections during the election cycle.

The next city election was coming up, so I was moved from the records area back to the elections area. Elections came in odd-numbered years, and there was not an entire election staff on board for the election years. People were "borrowed" from different divisions to make up the election staff during the election. My move back to elections wasn't long after being forced to move to another section because "I would not stop looking for a better paying position." I was now working my regular job and helping out with elections. I was moved back under the person that moved me because I wouldn't stop looking for another job!

After the election, the staff held a party for the workers and received a copper letter to thank them. I was not invited to the party nor given a copper letter. I was the only person working on the election not included in the party or award. They were all at the party when I heard about it. The party was at another location, so I wouldn't know they were having a party. When I asked why the staff did not include me, they told me I "did not work full-time" during the election. Working full-time in elections and continuing my "other full-time" duties was not "a realistic workload assignment." They used that argument to avoid inviting me to the party or giving me a copper letter. The election's boss was still mad that I had not stopped looking for a better job.

I was always struggling to make ends meet, and my friends knew. One worked at the Pima County Elections and knew of my work with the city elections. She asked her boss if I could help her with their early voting during the Pima County elections. Pima County held elections in opposite years as the city elections, so I would be free to help. He said that I could. My department head made a deal with the county that I would take my vacation from the city and make my city salary while working at the county, which the county would pay. It was a perfect deal for me. My friend ran the area each year and taught me everything she knew. I learned a lot about processing early voting ballots for counting.

To ensure the integrity of the elections, we had to know all the legal information, prepare all the forms, sort all the ballots into precincts, and supervise the processing of the ballots for the counting machines. They had to be ready for processing by a specific time on election night as they were generally counted first at the county. The city counted these ballots last. We had many people working on the boards for several weeks. Boards were set up just as at the polling locations, with five members on each board. The boards had one inspector who was a Republican on one board and a Democrat on the next to make the parties equal in participation. There were also two judges, one Republican and one Democrat, and two clerks, one

Republican and one Democrat. It was exciting and gave me an excellent extra income every other year, even though I used my vacation days.

My friend was in a women's religious group and asked me to join it. That is how I started getting more serious about my religion. It was a friendly group of moms and friends meeting in their homes. At one of the meetings, they asked if I had ever given my life to Christ, something I had never heard before, and I said no. They said they would help me do it and walked me through it. The minute I completed the words, I burst into tears and was very embarrassed. They calmed me down and said that there was nothing to be uncomfortable about and that some people reacted that way. Later I joined a nondenominational church where baptism was by total immersion. My daughter and I became baptized—again.

One night, as I was leaving the county after work and walking to my car in the garage a couple of blocks away, I felt like someone was following me. I walked up on the steps of the city building. The person walked past me, and I continued to the garage. The next thing I knew, they were behind me again. I didn't know what to do as there was no way to contact anyone. It was night, dark, and not in the days of cell phones.

As I was going toward the garage, a man came along, walking fast to the garage, and I intercepted him. I asked if he was going to his car and explained that I thought someone was following me. He said I should follow him. As we got to the garage entrance, he ran up the stairs and jumped over the railing to the next set of stairs. The man was waiting for me and ran away. The man I had requested help from chased the man following me, and then he took me to my car. That could have been very different had the man not come along. It was a very frightening moment and something that haunted me.

The next day, I wrote a note to city staff and said we needed some way to contact people in just these situations. The city put in a telephone, but they put the phone inside the garage! That didn't help as we had to go into the garage to make a call. At any rate, I believe that man saved my life. I didn't go to the garage at night alone again.

This experience solidified my being too scared to stay alone. In addition to this incident, we found one of our staff murdered at home. Our staff called her home because she hadn't come to work and was always punctual. Police were there, and she was dead. I was also a part of a group of entrepreneurs who had businesses and published a book listing our businesses. Most of our companies were based in homes with home addresses listed in the book. Another businesswoman listed in our handbook was also found dead. I had many reasons to be afraid to stay alone. It continues to this day.

I worked at the Pima County elections for several years on my vacations until they decided it was too expensive to use me. By this time, I was in charge of the whole operation at the county as the staff member I was to work with had moved on. I had moved up within the department in the city and was making more money, and it cost them more to hire me. Instead of using me from then on, they promoted the person I was training to assist me.

Experience with the Pima County elections came in handy several years later. Our department head called me into his office. It was a Wednesday between the primary and general elections. He explained that he wanted me to take over the early voting section on Friday—this was Wednesday. Until this time in my employment with the city, I was never involved in the absentee area. In addition, I didn't have the experience of already working the primary election. I had worked at Pima County on their early voting ballots but had never worked on early voting for the city. The new position was a much more significant part of the early voting process than I had done at the county—it was the entire process! It was like doing the work completed by the Pima County Recorder, an elected position. It was a little intimidating, and I told the department head that. He said he had confidence in me and that I would start on Friday. Okay! I was pleased he had so much faith in me, but it still was intimidating.

When others heard about my new assignment, they warned me about one employee they thought might cause me trouble. That was the least of my worries as I was the only permanent city staff member to work in the absentee or mail-out ballot section. Hereafter, I will use "mail-out ballots" to describe absentee voting. All the rest were part-time people. On Friday, my crew and I started the work on early voting. I was allowed to take my choice of one of the permanent employees from my division with me. I chose a person that I trusted to work well with me. Everyone questioned me about whom I chose, but I knew she was a good worker, and I could trust her without hesitation with this assignment. She was an excellent addition and completed all her duties exceptionally well. She became my second-in-command, and I think it pleased her to have someone have so much confidence in her.

As to the other employee they had warned me about, he became my third in command. He was a temporary worker, not a regular city employee with full benefits. When we got to work, he would say, "Sandy, today we have to teach the staff how to prepare the ballots for mailing."

And I would say, "And who does that?"

His answer was "You do!" He told me not to worry and that he would help me, and he did with everything.

I had to interview and hire at least twenty-five additional staff members. When I interview, I look for people with much experience, even if it is more than I have. I hire the most qualified! I don't worry about them being too competent. Some people in our department hired staff that didn't overshadow the supervisor. They usually ended up without the necessary skills. It put the supervisor at a disadvantage. People employed for clerical positions in our office did not have to pass a typing test! The first time I hired staff for a clerical job, everyone had to pass a typing test. It gave me an idea of how fast and accurate they could type. That only made sense!

We had many training classes, and the third in command helped me with them. This man warned me what to expect each day and got me through the ropes. All other staff members except the one I was allowed to take with me were temporary election staff. They usually worked for the city each election cycle and were well-trained in the Charter and Code requirements. That made the job a little easier.

With my second and third in command, we were quite a team. My two top staff members were my knot in the rope to hold onto in times of trouble. All the workers were behind me all the way. They were there no matter how many hours we had to work in a day. Of course, they made time and a half. I didn't. They were making more money than I was! That was my first role as mail-out ballot administrator for the city elections. It started with a bang, but we all pulled through it with flying colors. The department head must have been pleased because I moved to the section handling the mail-out ballots each election cycle until I retired.

During my first role as administrator of the section, the person I had replaced tried to find things incorrectly done. My staff told me he was in my office going through my papers and even removing some. They said he took the documents to the department head, who assigned me to replace him. He was trying to show that I was incompetent.

He also got the elections boss to set up a meeting with me. This person got the job "because she felt she owed it to him." I had no idea what was going on and was up to my "neck in alligators" that day. It was a meeting out of the blue, and I told the elections boss that I had to fix a problem first. He kept calling me. Finally, I was able to go to the meeting. The meeting was about not introducing new staff to the person I had replaced and not saying good morning when he came in. I asked him why he hadn't just mentioned it to me instead of at the meeting. I knew exactly what day he complained that I did not say good morning to him. That day I was walking down the hall, discussing a problem with a staff member. Instead of speaking, I shook my head, indicating good morning. It was nonsense to meet with the election's top staff member over this matter!

The department head did not call me into his office because of concerns about how I ran the mail-out ballots. He had seen my prior work ethic and trusted me completely. That made me confident.

During one election cycle, the ballot envelopes weren't going to reach us in time to type all the information on the envelopes. In the past, staff *typed* names and addresses on individual envelopes. But if the typist made mistakes, they had to retype the envelopes. It was a very tedious job. We're talking about thousands of envelopes. They had to be proofread more than once for accuracy of party and ballot type and all name and address information.

With the envelopes coming late, I had to figure out how to get the envelopes completed when the order came in. There was a set date in the City Charter and Arizona Constitution and statutes for mailing the information. I struggled at night trying to figure out how to make it happen. My religion came into action again, and I found and learned a computer program to print information onto forms using a database I knew how to use. However, you had to use a printer that printed continuously on paper. We didn't have such a printer in our area, and I didn't know if the city had one.

The department head knew of the problem that the envelopes would be late; however, she left a solution up to me. The department head had changed by now. It was up to me to find a solution. Politics in the office was getting worse for me.

When I figured out what to do, I told my division boss I needed a continuous feed printer and gave them time to find one in-house or rent one. It was a big machine, and there was no money, or time, to purchase such a printer. I bought the computer program with my own money and started to learn how to program it to print the information onto the form. But first, I had to program the database so staff could enter the information required for each ballot request. They entered the data while I learned how to program the printer. The information required for the database was a name, address, precinct, ward, dates, party affiliation, and other pertinent information. They could print the information from the computer and proof it ahead of time. The requests would be ready to print upon receipt of the envelopes.

My boss said they found an old continuous-feed printer and had it delivered. The information had to fit on the lines, which meant information had to be moved on the page by millimeters. I started practicing and finally had the forms printing perfectly. The staff was so excited because they were entering the names and proofreading as I figured out how to get the information on the forms. We had it all figured out by the time the order came in—what a relief. There was so much excitement in the office because we made lemonade out of a lemon. Everyone was excited about their part in the solution.

When the envelopes arrived, we put the forms in the printer and started it up! The printer ran continuously for at least thirty-six hours to get all the envelopes printed. Three of us stayed the entire time to watch the machine and ensure it didn't break down or that the paper went sideways. When they were all printed, the staff had to drive me home. Because of the stress and continuous hours, I was so sick with a migraine that I was a mess. But we had done it. The rest of the staff had been filling the envelopes, proofing them again, and getting them ready to mail as they were printing. Everything went out on time.

Most supervisors are good delegators. They tell staff what to do and how long it should take, then leave. That is not how I supervise. I don't believe in setting unrealistic deadlines and then leaving. If there is a deadline, I'm there helping staff get the work done, however long it takes. That's why I was there for thirty-six hours continuously.

An example of what a good supervisor does not do is what happened when we set up the first mail-out ballot office. My supervisor said to do it on a Saturday, and we should have it completed by noon. There was no way to set up an entire office for over twenty-five employees in four hours. We were there until it was done. The supervisor thought we should have been able to accomplish it faster!

It was a practice that the Democrats and Republicans asked for copies of the available information regarding ballots sent out and returned. We could only give information on how many mail-out ballots of each political party went out in the past because it was not computerized. That changed when we computerized the system because we didn't receive the envelopes on time.

One day, the department head called me on the telephone and said, "Sandy, can we get reports by Ward for Republicans and Democrats who have requested early voting ballots?" I assured her we could. And when I told her we could also get them by precinct, by ballots returned by precinct, by ward, by votes still out, and many other configurations, she was surprised. To be truthful, I was so proud of what we had accomplished that I wanted to say we could give them to her upside down! She was one who continually harassed me. Giving out these reports made her look efficient, and the parties were happy with the additional information. Each week they wanted new information, and we could give it to them.

This reporting system also made it easy to track the ballots as they came in and ensure they were accounted for when we turned them over for counting at the processing center. We included a report by party and precinct. The supervisor of the processing center kept telling me to turn the ballots over even if I could not provide a statement. If I did that, there would be no way for me to account for all the ballots. I was not willing to do this and jeopardize my position. They were agitated and threatened me to "just turn them over." It was more important to me to ensure the ballot count. They had to wait! My staff could account for all the ballots when we turned them over to the counting center. That is something the 2020 election was all about—voting integrity.

We provided all of these reports because the envelopes wouldn't make it to our office to mail ballots in the time required. We were able to take this significant problem and make some incredible things happen. Our staff had outdone themselves.

I hope this information on handling mail-out ballots was interesting to you. Now you know a little more about how you receive a ballot in the mail instead of voting in person.

Administrator Position

When I advanced in the ranks, I became an administrator over supervisors in several office sections. Previously, the supervisors were left
to their own rules, pretty much. For example, one supervisor gave
herself time and a half and allowed only one other staff member to
accrue overtime. She would not give out overtime to some of the
staff. Management also allowed her to come in before anyone else
was at work and work. However, she would not let others in her team
come in early because there was no one at work to check on them. I
had to counsel her that she had to give out the overtime equally to
everyone. It was a battle to get her to comply with the overtime. The
staff member who wanted to come in early changed her mind, and
this did not become an issue.

One of the supervisors believed that if she told a staff member
more than once about an error, she could discipline them in front of
the entire section. The first time I heard her harshly correct a staff
member like that, I called her into my office for discussion. She said
they deserved whatever she gave them if they didn't learn after being
told twice. More counseling!

This supervisor eventually was going to move to another state.
The department head was concerned that no one in the office could

do her job. This supervisor directed her staff through intimidation. I convinced the department head that we would not have a problem as I knew what to do except in one situation. I didn't know when he needed to sign a document or if the Assistant City Clerk could. He asked what it was and said it was no problem and that he could tell me what I needed to know. The problem was solved, and she left. I couldn't wait for her to move, and I believe her staff felt the same.

I would have continued to work at the department for many more years had I not run into politics in the office. The work in the city was gratifying and exciting at first. I loved my job and the many problems that I was solving. It gave me purpose and satisfaction. But it also put a mark on my back. My boss was getting ready to retire, and I was in the second position in our division and doing a good job. Therefore, I was a good replacement choice for his position. And that is where the politics came in.

I envisioned myself still working while in a wheelchair at seventy years old. I enjoyed the positions for about the first six years. When I started advancing, I could see the politics of the place. I could still deal with the politics until about the last five years.

The city had a policy that if the administrator or manager of a section was on leave, the person filling in received a raise of approximately 5 percent during the time they were taking on the extra duties. My boss usually went on military leave and vacations that lasted about two weeks each time. I was moved up the ranks and was finally able to take over for him when he was gone. I put in the paperwork for the raise, and the department head signed it.

A few days later, the department head asked me to put in the paperwork to give the raise to another employee. What? I told him that he had already signed paperwork for me to get the extra income. He said that he had promised that the raise would be rotated between two other staff members. Two people would be paid for the same thing if that paperwork were done. I told him, "I was doing the work." He was not happy! Neither was the one expecting the raise. It was the one giving me such a hard time. She was already making about twice my wages but was angry that she wasn't getting the extra income. That was the start of my problems with her.

My boss finally decided to retire, which gave me a great opportunity. However, the department head wanted another employee for the opening. By this time, there was a new department head. She gradually moved me to a much lower position in the division. She moved me from supervising the entire division to managing two half-time staff. I would come into the office and find a memo telling me I was now working in another area. In addition, the position of computer manager for the department I had applied for and was selected for was taken away and given to someone with little to no computer experience. I never knew what the next day would hold. The stress eventually led to a six-week medical leave.

Since taking my first computer class, I have loved working with computers and reading everything I could on computers. It was what I liked about the office. The only way I could deal with having it all taken away was to disregard anything to do with computers.

When politics enters the workplace, one thing that happens is that it gives others the freedom to also "play politics." People that I thought were my friends now felt that I was an open target, and they could also treat me differently. I learned who my true friends were, and there weren't many. That was a real eye-opener.

My brother worked in the police department as an officer and stopped trying for promotions. I asked him why. He told me he didn't apply because of the politics. I told him that I consistently applied and made them tell me I wasn't qualified. That stopped when I realized that there was no way I would ever get the job I was fully equipped for because someone else had already been "chosen." I understood what he was saying.

I also discovered that others get uncomfortable if you are religious and live your life that way. Talking about religion was not part of my upbringing; however, I did live my faith. They knew that I would not lie about an issue. If they intended to do something a "little unauthorized," I was never involved. If you have a giving personality, you can also set yourself up for others to take advantage of you.

Stress can bring on migraines, and I had terrible migraines. Others in my family also had migraines, such as my mom. We would get them for three days in a row. The pain would be so bad that it would upset our entire system. One of the prescriptions I took for migraines was Excedrin. It had codeine, and I didn't know that. I took too many at once and walked the floor praying because I had overdosed unknowingly on the medication. I couldn't breathe. Now, I tell the doctors that I am allergic to codeine, so they don't prescribe it. I am adding this knowledge in case your doctor prescribes this medication. You will know to be careful!

Top managers had to take turns preparing everything for the weekly governmental meetings. Typically, the deputy city clerk was in charge of these duties; however, the new city clerk did not appoint one. The work involved much mechanical equipment that I didn't know how to use. A large assembly was coming up that I was supposed to handle. I didn't want to admit not knowing how to use the equipment, but I also didn't want to mishandle the job. I knew it would throw me into a migraine, and I would be no good for anyone. I asked the other people doing the meetings if someone would change with me because I knew I would get a migraine. They laughed at me, and one finally agreed to switch to a meeting that was much more work. I didn't say anything but knew at least I wouldn't make a fool of myself. I wish I had told them in hindsight, but I doubt if they would have believed me. No one thought my headaches were that bad. They would say, "You stayed home because of a headache?" Only people who get migraines would understand!

My health deteriorated because of the harassment. Finally, my doctor told me I had to take six weeks off work. I told her I couldn't because the two half-time staff members were working on an election for their members, and I needed to be there for them. She said she had never heard of someone refusing to take time off if a doctor told them to. I told her I would call her and then go on medical leave as soon as the election was over. She agreed. She told me I wasn't to interact *at all* with the department head. I wasn't even going to that floor. My office was now on the first floor, and she was on the ninth floor. Okay, we understood each other. My staff took it upon themselves to go upstairs whenever needed.

When the time came, I went on medical leave, and the department head said she had no idea I was in such a condition. I tried to explain it to her, but she wouldn't listen. She denied knowing. I told her I didn't want to talk to her about it. She put me on "family medical leave," which was government jargon. I ran out of medical leave and asked for sick leave from my coworkers. She balked at it, but I told her that I had given others my paid sick time, and they could do it for me. They did. I was out for six weeks.

When I finally returned, due to the problems at city hall, I wanted to be placed at the Records Center in another building. The department head refused. Instead, she reassigned me to the Boards group in the basement. I was to take the place of a man who was retiring. He told me not to worry because his job only took about two hours a day. When I got into the position, I understood why he said that. I hadn't caught up with the backlog by the time I retired! He had not done much. Two hours would have covered his daily work.

There were six women I would supervise in a room with only one exit into another room with one way out. I asked management to install another door to make the space safe. For some unknown reason, management didn't approve this request. The room was in the basement and close to the garage exit. Someone could have come in and attacked all of us with no way out and no one realizing it. They could have easily left through the underground garage. To my knowledge, there is no other exit to this day. But there is no staff occupying that area.

The women accepted me as their new supervisor. By now, everyone was aware of what was happening to me. The staff I supervised was in the habit of attending meetings for overtime but just took time off, not asking for paid time and a half. That's how their former boss handled their overtime. I was not aware of this arrangement. The first time one of the women worked overtime, I asked for her overtime slip. She explained that their former boss didn't turn in overtime slips, but they took time off. I explained that the "law" said that everyone is paid time and a half after forty hours. And again, I asked for her overtime slip. I submitted the overtime slip to the time clerk as required. I didn't know that the time clerk didn't enter the overtime.

Because of the previous handling of overtime, I followed up to ensure the staff person had received her payment. The women didn't get paid for their overtime. I went to the time clerk and asked what had happened. She said the previous boss didn't allow overtime, and she hadn't put in the overtime slip. I was furious! The storm clouds over Tucson hit real fast! I asked her how she could change a form submitted by an administrator. She said she just did. From there, I went to *her* boss. He didn't like me interfering with his "payroll duties." But it never happened again. The time clerk did not have the authority to change a timecard made by an administrator. And her boss allowed her to do it. Both staff members believed they had the power to alter approved entries to the payroll.

The board's staff members also said they make time up for doctor visits. Their former boss didn't want to show any time used by his staff for sick leave. He bragged that his team hardly ever used sick leave. Now I knew why! That changed also. The time clerk's boss heard about that one also, and sick cards were turned in and reported on the payroll!

Time went on, and my boss retired. Management posted a listing of the position. I spoke with the department head regarding my desire to be considered for the job. She told me that I wasn't a good employee and didn't complete tasks, and so on. Evaluations didn't reflect these statements, and I asked her why. She said that no one wanted to hurt my feelings. My bosses had shown no displeasure with my work and had given me projects over and above my usual assignments. All of my evaluations were above standard. They were comfortable with the work I did. It was on time, correct, and usually beyond what they had requested. The statements from the department head were meant to discourage me from applying for the position. I left her office after one hour of this type of discussion.

I had already consulted an attorney, and he told me I could do nothing because I would be put on trial and lose no matter what. The wife was the head of one department, and her husband was second-in-command of another, and I couldn't win. I was fifty-seven at the time.

I decided it wasn't worth the agony to apply for the job for health reasons as I knew I wouldn't get it. The humiliation of listening to why I didn't get the job—because I wasn't a good employee—made me decide not to apply. The person they wanted for the job would get it no matter what, and she did. She even had the guts to call and ask if I had any ideas for what I would do if I got the job. I just said, "Yes"—nothing more. I continued my career wherever they put me. I did a good job, and on the day I reached "magic eighty," I retired. "Magic eighty" was when your age and the years you worked for the city totaled eighty. At magic eighty, you could retire with full retirement benefits.

Usually, the city provides good promotions to get higher-paying staff to retire early. There were no unique benefits when I retired, but I didn't care. My health was more important. I wasn't old enough to get social security, but I did get retirement benefits. I was working a second job, and my husband, whom I met at bowling, said we could make it without creating a money issue. So I retired and didn't look back.

When people retire, the office usually has a party. Top staff typically get more recognition at this time. My boss asked if I wanted a retirement party, and I said, "No, I would have one with my close friends." He asked if I wanted a copper letter, and I said, "Yes!" All retirees received copper letters upon retirement. I was bound and determined that they would not deprive me of this copper letter. I didn't want a retirement party with people who weren't my "friends." I didn't want to deal with people acting as if they cared when they didn't.

CHAPTER 17

Final Marriage

As the children grew up and graduated from high school, they began seriously dating and marrying one by one. My oldest son was married when I still was very short on money. Thankfully, the girl's parents paid for most of the wedding. I had a Certificate of Deposit from selling the land in Wisconsin. The company lets its clients use its venue at the top of the building for free. The venue looked out over the city and mountains. It was a perfect place for a wedding reception. I was able to use it and participate in the finances that way. I helped out in other ways but wasn't able to do much. Their father said he would help; however, he sent the money through the court, and they deducted it as child support. So it didn't help at all. I used the money for the wedding and didn't get child support.

My older daughter had already married at fourteen after becoming pregnant with our first grandchild. Her wedding was in the hospital as she had the baby, and we had a reception at our house afterward. She was happy, and that is all that counts.

By the time my younger daughter got married, we were a little better off, and I could help out more. The kids always asked me what I could afford to help them with and said they would cover the rest. Not many children are so mature and understanding while planning their wedding.

They had a beautiful wedding, and as the mother, I could do a lot more for her. Her oldest brother gave her away, and when the minister asked who "gives this woman," he said, "Her mother and I." I bought liquor at the Costco store every time I shopped so that by the time of the event, I had enough to cover a "no charge bar." My youngest and I were getting into this wedding. If I had a little extra money, we would go shopping and get something special. We decided to get a limousine for them, and we were like a couple of kids paying for it. It was exciting to be able to help more than before. None of the kids resented that I could do more for one than another. They understood. I wanted to give a toast to my daughter, her new husband, and I practiced for weeks. I do not like to speak in front of people, so that was a "biggie" for me. I think she was pleased. After that, I ensured all the kids had limousines when they married—even Sam's kids. It became our "thing."

Our youngest was married after attending some college in Phoenix. He was in a unique program where they were designing automobiles and was quite excited about it. However, he started working on a business project for himself and decided to quit college and start the business. It has been very successful for him and his wife.

Periodically, I would date for companionship. I met my *last* husband at a bowling alley when my girlfriend and I wanted to bowl but needed a team. After a gentleman stuck up for us, the new bowling alley accepted us. They tried to put us in a whole new team. That is how we got to that bowling alley in the first place. Another bowling alley stuck my friend and me on a new team by ourselves and expected us to get the other bowlers they needed. When we didn't, they said we couldn't bowl there. The gentleman at the new bowling alley said, "Hey, we need two on our team. Let them bowl here." Even though the teams were supposed to be equal between men and women, they allowed more women than men on our team.

The gentleman was kind, and we talked each week. He had a beard and looked very sharp. He wore Brut aftershave, which I am allergic to. I would be itching all night. Somehow, we mentioned the Brut, and I told him I was allergic to it. He never wore it again!

One night, he said, "Would you like to go out sometime?"

And I said, "Sure."

We bowled a few more weeks, and he said again, "Would you like to go out sometime?"

Well, I burst out laughing. He looked at me, and I said, "You already asked me that once and didn't do anything about it."

He looked sheepish and said, "Well, we will fix that tonight. When would you like to go out?" We made a date and started dating from then on. After a couple of years, we talked about whether we wanted to get married, but I wasn't very interested after my first two marriages. He wasn't in any hurry either, so we just continued dating.

We dated for five years, and I was still good with that, but he gave me a ring at Christmas of the fifth year. I opened the box and passed it all around the room. I thought it was a fancy ring because I loved rings, and he knew I did. When it got to my daughter, she said, "Well, Mom, what do you say?"

I was dumbfounded and asked to see the ring because we hadn't talked any further about getting married. You guessed it—a diamond engagement ring. So of course, my boyfriend gets down on one knee. Yikes! The answer was yes, but we had a long engagement until people started to ask, "When are you guys getting married?"

I was concerned about how I *would react* if my new husband told me we couldn't afford something like my ex had! I wasn't worried about my new husband, only that I wouldn't be able to compromise. I was concerned about my reaction if he said "no." We haven't had a problem! He doesn't say "no."

When we had finally set our wedding date, we discussed where we would live. My fiancé didn't like my house, and I didn't like his. So we sold both of our houses and bought a new one together. My fiancé went house hunting with the real estate agent and me for one day. Did I mention my fiancé was very impatient? After that day, he told the real estate agent to take me and let me find a house. The real estate agent found one he thought my husband would like because it had a workshop area. But I didn't like it because it needed much work to make it "home" to my liking. I didn't think we would have the money to fix it for several years. We were already in our fifties, and I didn't want to wait to fix it. The one the real estate agent thought my husband would like had a bedroom where the bed looked directly into the bathroom. I was not too fond of that arrangement and said so.

I found a home I wanted, but it was in a subdivision, and the home needed to be built. It took me about twenty-five years to realize that our bedroom overlooked our bathroom in the house we bought. Can't you see the real estate agent shaking his head because I had said I didn't want the bedroom to look into the bathroom on the other house? Indeed, he knew both houses were the same when I decided I liked the new one. I'm sure he said to himself, "Women."

My youngest son worked at Trail Dust Town, the cowboy steak restaurant in Tucson. If men wore a tie to the restaurant, they made a big deal about it and had all the waiters and waitresses come over and cut the tie off. People deliberately wore ties to "get the treatment." All the rooms have ties around the ceiling. They also had a gazebo that the employees could use for free, and my youngest son arranged for us to be married in the pavilion. It was very romantic. All the older sons, my fiancé had four sons; one was part of the wedding party, the rest took video pictures, my two sons took videos, and my brother took videos. We had lots of videos.

My oldest daughter was my matron of honor. My two little granddaughters, who were the same age, were dressed in the same off-white as I was. We had much fun at a later-in-life wedding. Afterward, we went to my house for the reception and just relaxed. The kids had control of the video cameras. As an afterthought, this was not a good idea.

A couple of nights later, my husband and I went through all the videos, enjoying the fun. All at once, I said to my husband, "What was that? Rewind the tape." He did, and there was a bare bottom in the picture! "Okay," I asked; which one of the kids thought it was funny to put their bare bottom on our wedding film, knowing it was one of his? I asked my husband if he recognized the bottom, and he said yes, it was his second oldest. That became his kids' tradition to show their butts at each wedding—until they did it in front of their grandmother! (That is when I was glad it wasn't one of my kids.)

By then, only one of our eight kids was still home, and it was my youngest son. He was ready for college. After our wedding, my husband rented a house for three months while they built our house. In 1992, during the high rent frenzy, people stood in line to rent any home at any price to get a rental. My husband had cash to pay, or we wouldn't have gotten the house. It was overpriced for what we rented!

We had to be out of my house the day after the wedding, and it was a Monday, so everyone was at work. I could take the day off, but no one else could. We hadn't packed anything because the reception was at my home, and we had just sold the house. The new owners wanted to move in immediately. I gathered boxes and boxed as much as possible, and all eight kids and significant others came over to help after work. I had a large freezer full of food and couldn't unpack it, or it would have spoiled. When the kids picked it up, they didn't know it was full, so it took six of them to get it out of the double windows in the family room and into the truck. They asked me why it was so heavy. They weren't happy when I told them it was packed—to the top. I asked them what I was supposed to do with the food while they were at work. No one answered. As they say in the movies, no one was hurt in this endeavor.

When we finally settled in that night, the kids had furniture on end throughout the house, stacking up to the ceiling. Imagine a four-bedroom home and another three-bedroom home packed into a small two-bedroom home. The house was full of furniture, including the shed out back. The kids left a pathway to the bedrooms and bath and a rocking chair sitting on our bed. You get the picture. There was no working stove, so we used a barbecue or electric fry pan. It was almost like camping. The water heater went out, and we had cold water to shower with. My son didn't know this little tidbit, and we heard unmentionable words when he showered the following day. The owner put in a used water heater.

When our house was ready, our real estate agent asked if we were still married three months later! He knew how we were living! We said yes and were so happy to move. All the kids showed up to "do it all over again!" Our home is at the end of the street and has a beautiful view of the mountains—something I missed while in Wisconsin.

I learned to choose my fights wisely. When my husband thought the toilet paper should be rolled around the top, which he did, and I felt around the bottom, which I did, was it worth a fight? I didn't think so. Toilet paper rolls over the top and has ever since. No problem.

The first Christmas, we had two trees—one for my kids and one for my husband's family. We decided to celebrate Christmas Eve with my husband's family and Christmas Day with mine. Christmas Eve came, and all the grandchildren on my husband's side came over. They were still young, and one was about six. The next thing I knew, he came to me and said, "Grandma, I checked all the packages under the tree, and there isn't one for me." I asked him if he had checked the Christmas tree in the family room. He said, "No," and ran off to do so. He came back with all smiles. He had found his gift.

I start shopping in August to save my sanity because we have many grandchildren and great-grandchildren. I can count on being complete by mid-October. Then it is only wrapping the gifts, which isn't so bad. There is also time to make the cut-out cookies that we all love. I make enough cookies to give to the two neighbors who help us and ensure we breathe daily.

Our Christmas was always a big deal with all the grandkids. On Christmas Eve one year, we were all opening gifts. I was getting them out from under the tree; some were in the back, so I had to lean over to get them. I held onto the rocking chair with my husband's mom in it when she turned the chair, and I went on my buns. The six-foot tree went flying, with all the decorations also flying. Everyone thought it was the funniest thing they had seen. It wasn't charming, but I survived. It has been the topic of Christmas discussion ever since. My name is not Grace!

I was in bed in the new home one day. I had a migraine when two men came to the door. My husband answered, and they were from a furniture company with a van full of furniture. They said they tried to deliver it to a furniture store, but the store wouldn't take it.

They went to new subdivisions and checked if anyone needed furniture for their new homes. We had a new home, so my husband woke me up. I went to the truck thinking we needed China cabinets

WE SURVIVED

for the good dishes. The cabinets on the truck were about four feet wide, and our wall was about nine feet wide. I explained to the men that one cabinet wouldn't be enough and that we would need two. They thought I was exaggerating. They came into the house and saw what I was talking about, and my husband agreed to buy two China cabinets. My husband then asked about a table and chairs to match the cabinets. The furniture was expensive and about half price. The men said yes, and my husband said that if they still had the table and chairs left before they went back to the factory, we'd maybe purchase them.

They came back.

I don't know if it was a good thing that my husband woke me up that day or not. He seems to think it was. We have some beautiful furniture in the dining area at a very reasonable price!

CHAPTER 18

Election Tech, City Clerk's Department

After retiring for several years, I returned to work on election night. The first year, I was to help with the provisional ballots. It was a new procedure, and no one knew the many steps. We worked until midnight, finally gave up in frustration, and came in early the following day to start again. And I do mean start again. Everything had been put in boxes and was not kept in a sorted fashion from the night before. It took at least one day to get the provisional ballots processed for the county recorder, who would then check signatures and send them back to the department for final processing.

A provisional ballot is issued to voters if their name is not on the registration rolls when they appear at the polling place. They complete a ballot, which is placed in an envelope to be processed the next day. The Pima County Recorder checks and verifies if they are registered to vote. If they are registered, the ballot is included with the regular ballots and processed. If they are not registered, the ballot is not counted.

The department head was upset with how the staff had handled the process. After the election, she hired me back to write procedures for the next election in two years. My task was to study the steps to process the provisional ballots and set up guidelines for the next election. After looking at everything, I wrote a computer program for the next election cycle. The program took the provisional ballots from the polling places to city hall for processing. It followed the ballots through several stations set up in the basement of city hall for processing until they were all processed and ready for delivery to the county recorder.

The program automatically printed a report at the end of the evening to be hand-delivered to the Pima County Recorder's Office the following day with all the ballots sorted by precinct. It was the first-time ballots had been delivered that fast. The election staff members were waiting for the County Recorder's Office to open the next day to turn over the ballots. Usually, the report and ballots took a couple of days of processing time for completion.

The report gave the department head a record of ballots throughout the evening, what precincts were in, what precincts weren't in, and where the ballots were in the processing cycle. Previously, she asked for information whenever she wanted a report. That would not work for me because there were ballots at several stations, and we needed time to compile a report for her.

Because I was not a permanent employee, I asked her staff to request a timetable from her. They said they couldn't ask her that; *she just told them* when she needed it. That wasn't going to work for me, so I asked her myself. I showed her what the program did and why I needed the timetable. She was pleased with how the program would operate and knew the program would give her up-to-date information whenever she wanted. She readily gave me her schedule—every two hours, beginning at a specific hour. It was an exciting accomplishment for a "retiree," primarily because this was the woman harassing me so much.

When I had a problem writing the program and went to our in-house computer staff for the solution, they didn't know a program could do what I had done. These computer staff had a college degree, and I didn't. Good thing I didn't realize it wasn't possible. Anyway, they were able to help me when I explained what I was doing, and I completed the program. It's funny what you can do when you don't know any better.

During this time, I also received an assignment to check the reports filed by candidates showing their money raised and spent during the campaign cycle. These reports were required by law. The department had a computer program to review these forms, but I was supposed to do a final report. Candidates file these reports several times during an election. Our city is divided into six wards. Candidates for six wards and the mayor's position are elected in odd-numbered years, two years apart. One year we select the mayor and three ward candidates, and the next time the other three wards are elected. These reports cover at least three wards with candidates in specific years and at least six wards with the mayor's position in different years. Each ward can have several Republican and Democratic candidates.

There have been many reports filed! I was breezing through them when, all at once, one of the reports didn't make sense. I checked everything several times and came to the same conclusion each time. There was a "bug" in the computer program. In other words, there was an error in how the program computed the reports. The city had been using this program for several years already. No one had discovered the error. So when I had to go in and tell the department head this news, it did not go over well. I had all the examples of why the program didn't work. She agreed. The next day, the computer staff was working to correct the problem.

It is not unusual to find a "bug" in a program. The computer staff writes a program, but the people using the program do not take the time to check it thoroughly for errors. I use a program for taxes, and every time it updates, it cannot find the connect-up report. It drives me crazy. When I get a notice that the program has been updated and is ready for me to download, I want to say, "Noooooooooooo!"

CHAPTER 19

My Business

Our marriage fit in nicely with both our jobs and my second job. My second job was Cooking the American Way and Christmas Around the World party planning. The training was in California, where my director lived. I started the business before our marriage. Money was scarce, so my fiancé would drive me overnight to San Diego for training while I slept. We would stop at a McDonald's or restaurant with a public bathroom when we got to San Diego, where we would eat breakfast, and then I would go into the bathroom and get into my "meeting" clothes.

While I was at training, my fiancé would sleep so he could drive me home right after the training. This way, we didn't have to rent a room overnight and would get home in time to return to work on Monday. Both had gotten the necessary sleep. My director finally said she would pay for our room so we could stay overnight. That was such a relief, and I got to know the women in our group and became fast friends with many of them.

During one summer during my supervisory years in the group, my mom and I took a trip from Tucson across the United States to South Carolina. Mom went with me because I didn't want to go alone—no surprise, right? I was still not comfortable doing things alone. I had about eight supervisors that needed training in my group in various states. The company gave us money to train people in other areas and travel to them. On the morning of our departure, I got up with a migraine. Nothing new. I started driving. When I got to Mom's, I put the luggage in the vehicle. I got as far as the road in front of her house. I pulled over and threw up in a plastic bag. Migraines did that to me. My mom looked at me frantically and said, "Are we still going?"

Nonchalantly, I said, "Yes," and we continued the trip.

The women were about a day's drive away from each other, and we would pull into the city where the first one lived, and I would pull out the training manuals I had prepared for each of them. The training would take place, and we would stay the night in that city and leave for the next town the following day.

In one of the cities, the woman had a very young child, and she looked through all my supplies while I trained her mom. She was such a little cutie. I recently made contact with the now young woman.

In New Orleans, we decided not to stay in a motel because we were on the streets of the French Quarter. We felt it was safer to stay in a hotel as I was concerned about leaving my car out front. The hotel had free parking in a garage, and the car was safe.

We found all the women quite quickly, except for the last stop in South Carolina. I finally called the woman and asked if she and her group could meet us at the motel instead of driving to them. They were happy to do so. We had dinner, and then I did the training. My mom fell in love with the group members, and they loved her. They asked about my mom throughout our time in the business. People got along very quickly with my mom.

Driving to one of the cities, we became lost. Now that wasn't unusual for Mom and me when we went anywhere. We would get lost at least once. And when we would get going in the right direction, we would laugh and say, "Now that is over for this trip." We found ourselves driving in a lane.

Mom kept saying, "Sandy, I think we are lost." We decided it was confirmed when we encountered a farmer driving a tractor in a field. He saw us and came over to see what we were doing in his lane.

We laughed and said we were lost. He said that he gathered that and helped us get back to the road and on our way.

Mom and I had a lot of fun on that trip. We always had fun when we did anything together because there was always an "oops" on the trip.

We were required to attend yearly meetings at the company headquarters in Kansas City, Kansas. The ones earning awards were honored by walking across the stage and saying a few words. The first time I did that, I said my name and told them I was a senior citizen instead of a senior supervisor. They all laughed, and I said, "What did I say?" When they told me, I had to laugh and tell them that I was that also, but I wasn't.

Another time, I told them how to remember my name. One of the men at my regular work didn't like me very well, and he referred to me as "Fat-o-bitch." My name is Fatovich. One of the people in the district office, my friend, told me what he was calling me. So I just thought, *Okay, I will make a joke of it*, and that is what I did. At the yearly meeting, when I introduced myself, I explained that they could remember my name by thinking of "fat-o-bitch" and then changing the *b* to a *v*, and it's Fatovich. It took his power away from him. The audience said, "Ohhhhh," and then we all laughed. But I bet they always remembered my name.

You have probably noticed that I repeatedly remark, "And we laughed," throughout the book. It wasn't easy to do during my first marriage, and it was liberating after the divorce. We were able to laugh easily—the kids and me.

At one of the yearly meetings in Kansas City, Kansas, the company announced a new line of products, including teddy bears. After the training meeting, we were all given one of the largest teddy bears to take home. All the women got on the airplanes holding giant teddy bears. It caused quite a reaction on the plane. I still have mine.

The women were devastated when the company was sold after the owner's passing. The new owners put us into bankruptcy within a short period of time. We had such a fantastic company, and they treated us well. We had many perks for a home-based business. The women still get together on Facebook.

On one of the trips outside the continental United States, one of the woman's husbands passed away. Quietly, the company paid for a ticket for the woman and a top staff member to go to her hometown and take care of anything the woman needed. When the woman was okay, the staff person returned to the trip, and no one knew what had happened. They took care of that woman's needs. They treated us like children because most of the women had never traveled. Most had a second job to increase their insufficient income. It was an excellent way to "start traveling" when you had never done it before.

Throughout the year, the company would have contests company-wide, and everyone would have contests for their group of workers and the hostesses. There would be prizes for top sales each period by the hostesses and the workers. Some hostesses held parties with about one thousand dollars in sales.

I contacted the workers in our group each month with newsletters and the hostesses with notices or booklets with cooking ideas. The cookbooks had one food item highlighted in each brochure. For example, all cookies, pies, bread, et cetera, could be kept so they could only go to one book for cookies, pastries, et cetera. The booklets were five and a half inches by eight inches and easy to handle. It was a way to show the people I cared.

Before we married, the money helped pay the bills. After our marriage, the extra income from this second job was our "cushion" to purchase furniture and other things we needed but didn't want to buy with our regular income. The company always held our last check from November and December, and we would get an extensive paycheck about December 12–15 each year. These checks were between two thousand and four thousand dollars depending on our sales. We used them to buy items on trips or beautiful furniture that I would never have believed possible. These large paychecks also paid for our big purchases, such as built-in bookcases in Grandma's room, a pier bedroom set for us, and unexpected expenses.

At Christmas, our catalog always had unique dolls. We had several artists on staff who designed our product line. I love dolls and had over one hundred at one time. I have since given most of them away to my grandchildren, other children, and people who love dolls. The Gospel Rescue Mission in Tucson helps needy families, and I gave them dolls for the children. I still have about thirty. I also gave one large doll to the Ronald McDonald House in Tucson. They have a house where families can stay for free while their children are ill in Tucson. I told them they could give the doll to a child if needed.

While working for the company, one of the large dolls came with a broken leg. We always had to give damaged items to a charity. If we delivered the items to a charity, we didn't have to return the products or pay for them. The company allowed me to deal with a company that made artificial limbs for injured people. They made a leg that was removable from the doll and was authentic. They made it free of charge. We gave it to a little girl in Mexico who had lost the same leg. I was not able to be there when she received the doll.

The news media gave us the newsreel of the little girl getting the doll but wouldn't mention the company because they considered it advertising. I sent a copy of the newsreel to the company. The little girl was so excited to get the doll. She was probably about ten years old.

Each year, the second job grew more significant, and eventually, we sold enough products to earn a free trip. The first one always was Hawaii, per the company's rules. When I acquired the first trip, my mom asked me what I would do. At that point, I was still scared to do anything alone because of the verbal abuse—"You're too dumb, you're too stupid, what makes you think you can do that, et cetera?" Thankfully, I decided that I would go. Had I not gone the first year, there was a chance I would forgo the trips after that. Don't let the words of an abuser continue to control your future.

We could substitute money instead of going on trips, but most people's trips were the "frosting on the cake." No one else from Tucson was also traveling with the company that first year, so I had to make the trip alone. I was so scared that I was shaking and, as usual, got a migraine headache.

We got to California, where others met me in our district, and we traveled together from there. Company trips always were free as we had earned them through product sales. We would receive our tickets in the mail, all paid. Our rooms were paid for and were in four- or five-star hotels. The company also paid for our meals. The company made sure desserts were available at every meal. These trips were popular with the women because most were in the low- to middle-income range and couldn't afford to travel. The women worked for extra money, making the trips unique to us. Leis were put on us as we arrived in Hawaii. Quickly, I learned that all we had to pay for were our purchases. After that, we would save all year long to spend freely on "our purchases."

That first trip wasn't as exciting as it should have been because I was so scared all the time, even though the company watched out for us and scheduled places for us to go. We went to significant sites in the country (in this instance, a state). We traveled together by bus rented by the company. We were taken care of for the entire trip, but going alone was scary for me on the first trip. The company had arranged for us to go to a luau. We had roasted pigs from a pit, and they had dancers. One of our workshops was learning the hula. Another was making leis. We had to attend three training days as part of our "free" trip requirements. No one complained!

We all went shopping when not in training. The last night was awards night, where all award winners walked across the stage and were honored with pins or plaques. The top three positions each received a tiara and a dozen red roses for the highest sales and top overall group sales.

It seemed like the women couldn't get enough shopping done, and we were out shopping the day of the awards night. The women I was with shopped until we discovered the buses to take us back to the hotel had stopped for the night. One of the ladies talked to a school bus driver, who graciously took us back as the kids were no longer on the bus. We were able to get dressed in time for the special night. Can't you see all of us women on a school bus?

We could earn free trips on our sales and our group's sales. After the first few years, our group made so many sales that others joined me, and finally, I earned two to three free trips a year. The company took me to Honolulu, Hawaii, in 1992, and Acapulco, Mexico, in 1993. In 1995, we went to Maui, Hawaii. We went to Germany and Austria in 1996, Greece and Turkey in 1997, and New Zealand and

Australia in 1998. On the New Zealand–Australia trip, my husband could finally go on as our group had so many sales. I made several other trips before the company went bankrupt.

It seemed like I always wanted to grow any business I was building. I looked for ways to get ahead. I decided one way was to have a website for my group. Not knowing anything about building one, I checked out having one built. The Trump University held a seminar in Tucson, and I went. There were several seminars in Phoenix and Tucson, and hundreds of people attended.

I signed up to have a website built for five thousand dollars based on the name recognition of Mr. Trump. While I waited for them to make the website, they offered a class in Phoenix that Mom and I attended on building a website.

As time went on, nothing happened with the website. I contacted the people, and they just put me off. For months, nothing happened. When I reached the Trump Organization, they notified me that they had given their name only and weren't involved. As so many people from Arizona were losing money, I contacted the Attorney General in Arizona. The Attorney General did nothing. With so many people losing money, I couldn't believe they did not do anything.

Being out five thousand dollars, I decided to use the information from the classes in Phoenix and build the website myself. The classes were excellent, and I created a unique website. There were pages for games for children, tips for hostesses, and all fifty states, with our group members added to their respective states. People could go to their state and see if there was a representative to hold a party for them or recruit them into the business. I obtained an 800 number so my group and others could call me for free. The website had over seventy-five pages when it was complete. I figured I got something for the money I spent—even if I had to build the website myself.

The first cruise I earned was to Greece, and the women told me that the "cruise" was on a small ship, not the cruise liner you would typically imagine. The ship traveled while we were sleeping, and I went to the restroom one night. The ship was rolling so badly that I couldn't get off the toilet without pulling on the washbasin. I started laughing at the predicament so hard that I woke up my roommate. She didn't think it was funny.

We went to two islands, Santorini and Mykonos, while staying on the big island of Greece. The water surrounding the islands was a beautiful blue.

Mykonos is an artists' haven, and we all couldn't wait to go there. We knew we would miss the trip back to the cruise ship if we weren't back at the dock at a specific time. I was still very timid about traveling and stuck close to the other women. The other women had been on so many different trips that they took everything in stride. They wanted to go check out the whole island, and when it became close to the time we were supposed to be back at the dock for the trip back to the ship, we were helplessly lost. The scenes were gorgeous, and it is no wonder artists came there. The women didn't think anything of the fact that we were lost. They had been on many trips with the company and weren't worried. I was horrified. We made it back to the dock just as the last boat was getting ready to leave back to the ship.

We discovered you reached Santorini by riding donkeys up a steep road. Some women didn't want to or didn't feel comfortable riding donkeys, and the company had a different means for us to get up the winding road. My mind wasn't on riding donkeys up such a steep road. I don't remember how the company got us up there—but they did. The company always had any problem imaginable covered. While walking around, we found beautiful white buildings with blue-domed rooftops and blue windows and doors and just had to take pictures. The scene was gorgeous. I don't remember much about Santorini besides the islands' beauty and serenity.

We stayed on the cruise ship docked on the main island of Greece. While there, we saw the site of the first Olympics. Like children, we ran up the steps and took pictures of each other. They also took us to underground tunnels found in an ancient city. The men used these tunnels to go and see their "other" women.

Turkey was a side trip we took. We were told to leave our checks on the boat and only take cash. We saw only men shopping in Turkey, no women. The store owners would pull on our arms to get us into their shops. It was very unsettling. I found a wallet to get for my husband and, in purchasing it, discovered that the smallest bill I had was a hundred-dollar bill. I gave it to the owner of the shop. One of the clerks grabbed the money out of my hand and ran. I figured that was the last time I would see that one-hundred-dollar bill.

Someone saw me distressed and asked what was wrong. The shop owner told me, "Not to worry; the man would be right back." That didn't make me feel all warm and fuzzy. But the man did come back. He said he had to go to the bank to cash the bill for change. No one had money to make change in their stores, and it was a regular trip for them to go to the bank, cash the money, and bring back change. Whew! What a relief!

The rug prices were fantastic in Turkey, and many women were taking advantage of that fact and purchasing rugs. They were oversize rugs. Try to imagine getting these rugs on an airplane! The shop owners told the women they could ship them home from Turkey. The shop owners usually planned the shipping for foreigners who bought their rugs!

Our trip home was quite eventful. There was a storm, and we couldn't get out of Greece in time to meet our connection in the United States. We got to New York and had to stay overnight because we missed our connecting flight. They gave us vouchers for food and rooms. I had a room to myself and hardly slept, afraid I wouldn't wake up to get back to the airport for the flight. We finally made it back to Tucson, and I could breathe a sigh of relief. I never was afraid like that before the mental and physical abuse, and when I was divorced, it took quite a while to get back to not taking things so seriously.

When I started working with the company, I was not married. My mom always picked me up from the airport. I would meet her dragging my luggage, looking like a wiped-out rag. She laughed every time. She knew I had enjoyed the trips but was glad to be home again. The trips were full of activities, and we were tired when the trips were over. But we wouldn't have it any other way. We loved those trips!

By 1998, my district manager was promoted to regional manager, and I became a district manager. My group sales were earning me two or three free trips a year. I could go to one of the destinations using the trips or even two trips. We also could take others if we had earned more than one trip.

CHAPTER 20

Major Trips Earned

My group sales in 1998 earned me three trips, and the major trip for higher sales was to New Zealand and Australia. My husband didn't go with me until this time because I didn't earn a second trip. He wasn't anxious to fly anyway and didn't care. But the New Zealand and Australia trip changed his mind. He asked for time off from work, and his boss said he couldn't take two weeks' vacation simultaneously. His boss said his job wouldn't be there if he went. My husband thought this over and decided it was too great an opportunity and that he was willing to forgo his roofing job to go. He told his boss he was going on vacation as he would never have such a chance again. (His position was there when he got back.)

The trip was very long, with a stopover in Hawaii. It was just in and out at the airport. It was enough that my husband could say he was in Hawaii.

The only time the company could make arrangements, considering the weather, was during the Easter holiday. We got to New Zealand first, and I told my husband we had to go "shopping immediately." We had to "get him with the program" as he wasn't one to shop. That turned around fast. Because the company paid for everything, he didn't mind shopping when confronted with it. While I was in the training meeting, he went shopping and got some of the things I had seen but felt were too expensive. He went back and bought them. What a sweetheart this one was! We have a large clock made of their "trees" that is beautiful and expensive. He bought it!

At the first meeting in New Zealand, we listened to the speaker when there was a commotion outside. After the training meeting, I told my husband, and he said, "Yes, that was me. I was trapped in the elevator." They would talk with him in the elevator and tell him they were trying to get him out. What an initiation of his first trip. He was the excitement of the day and took it very well. He puffed out his chest! All the women on the trip wanted to hear all about it.

We went to the site of the first bungee jump, and some of the group decided to take the bungee jump themselves. They thought it was exhilarating. I would have yelled down and then back up. I cannot even ride a roller coaster.

The company had made arrangements for us to visit the zoo. The buses were running late, and the zoo would be closed when we arrived. The company staff called the zoo headquarters and arranged for them to stay open for us. Yes, the company did have pull.

From New Zealand, we flew to Sydney, Australia. Busses took us to the Sydney Opera House, where the conductor was ready to teach all of us to play in "the orchestra." We went to the orchestra seats, and on each seat was an instrument. These were not the instruments used in an orchestra. They were the kind of instruments kids played with, such as triangles, maracas, rhythm sticks, kazoos, and tambourines. We practiced and had to play our instruments when the conductor pointed at us. It was fun and unusual. I can see him going home and saying to his wife, "You will not believe what I did today!"

This trip was when they were preparing for the Olympics the following year, and we got to see the Olympic pools for the swimming events. We all put our feet in the water to say we did. We could say we were there the following year when we watched the Olympics.

While in Australia, the company had a contest for the best "Easter hat," as it was the Easter holiday. We all got busy designing our "masterpiece." My husband went with me to get the supplies. I told him I wanted a stuffed rabbit and would put it on the hat upside down. He asked why, and for the life of me, I couldn't figure out why—I just knew it had to be upside down. Afterward, we realized that the upside-down bunny represented Australia as "down under." The "bonnet" won the first prize, a large bouquet.

We stayed at my stepson's home during a training trip to Utah. It was a three-story home. We took our dog, Tuffy 2. He was named Tuffy 2 because I had a Tuffy 1 that passed away and looked exactly like Tuffy 2. The family thought that was funny. None of our dogs knew how to walk up steps as we had a one-story house in Tucson with no entrance steps. We got to their home, and everyone came rushing to meet us. We hadn't seen them for some time. Sam and I ran up the steps to hug everyone. We turned around, and Tuffy 2 was at the bottom of the steps. He didn't know what to do. We tried to coach him up the steps. He didn't know what the steps were. My husband finally went down and carried him up the steps. We had to carry him up and down the stairs from then on.

One day, my daughter-in-law decided to teach Tuffy 2 how to go up and down the stairs. She sat on the stairs a little way down. We were at the top and sent Tuffy 2 down. She was going to catch him. Oops! She didn't. He slid on his tummy to the bottom—there were quite a few steps. We all just looked at each other. At the bottom of the stairs, Tuffy 2 shook his head. That was the end of that lesson.

My oldest son finally trained Tuffy 2 to go upstairs and downstairs when they were dog-sitting. He had quite a long training session. But Tuffy 2 graduated.

An Alaskan cruise was our trip destination in 1999. Again, our group earned me three trips. My husband, my mother, and I took the three trips we earned. We asked my husband's mom to go along, and my earnings paid for her trip. I had only earned three trips but could purchase another if needed.

The staff directed us to our next boarding station at the Washington airport. Unfortunately, it was wrong when we arrived, and we had to hurry to the correct one. The elderly moms weren't as fast as us, and I went ahead while my husband stayed with the moms and got there just as the doors were closing. They wouldn't open the doors to let us board the plane.

I had to call the company headquarters and tell them we had missed our flight. They got us on the next flight. Because we were late, we almost missed the cruise liner. On top of that, the cruise ship staff mixed up my mom's boarding pass, and their team took her off the list. The trip director had to help us get that straightened out. We were the last passengers to board. When we got to the ship, my husband's mom said, "Oh, my!" That was her favorite statement. She was impressed! It made us so pleased to be able to do that for her.

They placed the two moms in one cabin and my husband and me on another level. I asked if we could be placed side by side, and the trip director said, "Sandy, you don't want to do that." They showed us our rooms. The mom's cabin was a standard issue. Our cabin was on the outside with a window, large with all the amenities. The trip director was right; we didn't want to change rooms. High-trip earners had exquisite rooms! You had worked hard to earn that trip, and no one ever gave up the best rooms.

As usual, the company had everything assigned by day, with our three mandatory workdays, and the rest was port calls, trips to Alaskan villages, and salmon fishing for my husband. We could make special arrangements so the men could fish. I made the arrangements ahead of time. The men were excited to go fishing, and the women went shopping. My husband said his group was on the worst-looking boat, but they were the only ones that caught any fish. We had a wonderful time, and the moms were happy to have the trip. It was fun for us to be able to give it to them.

The meals were delicious. My husband is a small-built man but can eat anyone under the table. One night we had lobster, and he kept asking for more. We could eat as much as we wanted on any of our trips. He took advantage of it! They probably thought he had a hollow leg.

We saw whales swimming and ice glaciers with ice falling into the ocean, and we could name a mountain peak. We found an unusual peak that we named Sandy. When anyone saw whales in the water, word went around the ship. We all wanted to see whales. It took a couple of times before we could get to the railings to see the whales.

Enough company field workers earned trips for the Alaskan cruise for which we filled one ship and one-half of another one. The Alaskan cruise was only one of the three trips available for trip earners. That gives you an idea of how many people earned trips each year. The company was big and made it possible for many people to earn trips.

The year 2000 found us in London and Ireland on our trips. Again, our group had sold enough products for three tickets. This was one of the significant trips, and we needed double product sales for better journeys. Our group sales earned two people one week in London and one person an additional week in Ireland. To enable my husband to go with me to Ireland, I paid for the fourth trip. We made many new friends, and some traveled to Ireland with us.

They lost our luggage on the way to London, and the people on our trip knew we were without luggage. Each day they would ask, "Did your luggage come?" They realized we hadn't because I was wearing slacks and shirts each day instead of dressing up for the training and sightseeing the company had organized.

I was acting a little silly by the third day about not having clothes as it was getting funny, and I would strut across the stage in my slacks where the other women were in fancy dresses. We tried to make it fun and not an issue. Other men were offering my husband some underwear, which he denied.

It was getting close to the awards night, and we still didn't have our luggage. My husband wanted me to go shopping for a fancy dress to wear. With the hamburgers' price, there was no way I was going shopping, and I told him so. Prices were so high that we had lunch in the hotel one day, and my husband ran out of money in his wallet. He always carries lots of cash, so we were shocked at the prices. I looked in my purse and found enough to pay for the rest of the meal. That is why I wouldn't go shopping. I would have walked across the stage in my slacks. That is when the luggage came. It came just before we had to leave for Ireland!

Our hotel was next to Queen Elizabeth's palace, and we could walk past it. The bus took us past the Queen's Guard's changing shifts. We were in London when there was a disturbance, and our hotel was locked. That is why we ate hamburgers at the hotel—we couldn't leave.

The company arranged for us to visit the Queen's country home and tour parts of it. We saw where the palace had burned a few years back and had to undergo significant construction to repair it. My husband tried to take a picture of the castle, but so many people were standing around that all he got were heads. So he said into the video camera, "And this is the heads of the people."

As usual, we all went shopping. My husband was "with the program" by now, enjoying shopping with the rest of us. While there, we noticed a play was showing about *The Buddy Holly Story* and *The Big Bopper*, JP Richardson. Having never been to a show of this magnitude before, I bought tickets as a surprise for my husband as he loved Buddy Holly, and so did I. The play was fantastic. It was late when the show closed.

London taxis had lined up to take all the theatergoers back to their hotels. My husband went to a driver who was not in the taxi line. This man still took people to their hotels, but he was not a taxi driver. We got in, and the driver drove so fast and down back streets that I was scared to death. Were we going to end up in an ally dead? Quietly in the back of the car, I told my husband that I would hurt him badly if he ever did that again. I was *mad*. We ended up safely at our hotel, and the man drove off fast to take another group to make as much money as possible.

The awards night came, and we had our luggage. So I could walk across the stage at the awards dinner in an elegant dress like the other women. We had a fabulous dinner, and the company staff announced we were taking a small break. Everyone ran to the bathroom and back, not wanting to miss the entertainment. Everyone was ready with their cameras because this entertainment was going to be extraordinary. We weren't disappointed.

At the appropriate time, the doors opened, and Queen Elizabeth's horses and riders came through the doors. Everyone just went wild. At least eight to twelve horses and riders were doing fancy footwork around our tables. Lightbulbs were flashing everywhere. It was the most incredible experience any of us had ever had. We talked about it for days. Can you imagine the pull that the owner must have had to accomplish this entertainment for us?

The next day, we were on our way to Ireland. The country is beautiful, so green. By this time, I was a lot more comfortable in my skin. When we went to a pub, the guys got pints of beer and glasses for us women. I said, "No way, I wanted a pint." I wanted to say that I had a "pint" of beer in a pub in Ireland. That experience was essential to me. Funny what turns our world.

While in Ireland, we went to a unique tourist attraction. I had a terrible migraine as usual and wasn't going to miss this outing. I went to the back of the bus and lay across the back seat. My husband sat next to me. When the driver was ready to leave, he asked about the woman in the back and if she was going with us. My husband said, "Yes," and off we went. The migraine didn't go away, but the sights were fabulous. It was well worth the misery to be there.

We also went to a river dance at a large pub, and halfway through the dance, the lights went out. There was a storm, and the building went black. It didn't take too long, and somehow, they had the lights back on. We loved to see the dancers do the River Dance. It was so awesome. Irish living must be fun all the time. That is how the people made us feel.

The doors to the homes in Ireland are all very bright and have different colors. They paint the doors differently, green, red, and orange, so the men can find the right door when they come home drunk. I wonder, Who thought of that?

The last trip I was able to take was back to Hawaii. The Hawaiian trip is usually only for the new trip earners. But I couldn't go to Egypt—the trip I should have been on—because my stepson was getting married when we would have been there. The Hawaiian trip was at a different time and allowed me to go there. I loved Hawaii and had no problem going a third time.

Each time I took a trip, I would bring a gift home for each person in my group that had worked hard, and as a result, our sales earned me trips. Some women in my group also sold enough products for trips for themselves. However, trip sales were high, and you had to be very serious, or it didn't happen. It got to the point where our group was so big that I could no longer afford to get each host-ess a gift. So I started getting coins from the trip destinations and brought them back to have something to give them from the trip.

CHAPTER 21

New Company

At the end of each year, I would have two big parties. One was for our sales group, and I gave out prizes for top sales, recruiting, et cetera. The top salesperson received a dozen red roses and a tiara (because I always wanted one, I made sure my women got one). I recruited across the United States, and the winner might be in another state. Wherever the winner was, I would call the woman's husband and arrange for him to pick up a dozen red roses and send the tiara and money to him to present to her. I tried but was never able to recruit in Mexico. I couldn't speak Spanish, which made recruiting more challenging.

The second party was for my hostesses, who took the time to have parties for our products and helped me earn my trips. We set up a Christmas tree that was all decorated. My sales force from Tucson helped me with this party. All the products I didn't need were wrapped in Christmas paper and under the tree. Items ranged in price from the lower end, and then there were products, like dolls, that were one hundred dollars or more. There were many presents. I wanted to reward my hostesses instead of selling the products to people who didn't have a party.

We had food and played bingo, and we just had a great time. Whenever someone yelled "Bingo," they chose a present from under the tree. We wrapped the packages, so no one knew what they were getting—big or small. The women were excited to participate because many went home with more than one gift. We took pictures of everyone who got a gift. Everyone got at least one present. They received a gift anyway if they didn't get bingo at the night's end. My hostesses were always ready to do it again the next year.

Our last trip with House of Lloyd, Inc. was supposed to be a Caribbean cruise, and of course, we all wanted to go. I had learned to love cruises. However, the owner had passed away, and the adult children decided they would have to sell the company. They spent many months finding the right new owners.

We all started working for the new company. It was different. The new company made changes, and while they assured us everything was going well, orders started getting slower. It was getting a little uncomfortable explaining why the products weren't arriving as quickly as before. Finally, I told my group not to send in any more orders. The new owners were taking the money but not sending out the product. Our hostesses expected prompt service, and they were complaining. I ensured all my hostesses got their product or their money back. They had been dedicated to helping me in my business, and I didn't want them to suffer.

The new owners finally acknowledged to the field workers that they were going bankrupt but not before taking everything of importance from the company. We believe it was the plan from the beginning. The new company wanted the unique sorting machines. Afterward, we found out they had done this to other struggling companies. It shocked the former company's children because they had tried hard to keep us all working and with a good company. The children apologized to all of us. They were embarrassed by what had happened.

The new company didn't honor our trips and gave us products instead of money. That is just what we needed—more product. However, if we wanted to get the money coming to us, that is the only way we could get it and hopefully sell it to get our money. Of course, that didn't happen. The women who had received an excellent extra salary from the former company and loved the trips went into a deep depression. I retired based on this income. It was so sad for all of us. We loved the original company, how they had made better people of us and given us extra income and those beautiful trips that we would never have had.

A third company tried to put us back to work, but it didn't work out. They didn't have the same rapport with the women and changed too many rules regarding how we worked and reported. They changed the products, along with many other things. The company finally failed, and we were all out of work again. I tried one more company but eventually gave up. By then, I was getting older and was trying to help my mom and sister, who needed extra help.

Life went on without a second job. I was very depressed. My husband and I were getting along fine without the income; however, it was tight.

Our kids were all on their own. We had our pet "as our child." We had two male dogs that looked almost identical, and I named them Tuffy 1 and Tuffy 2. Tuffy 1 lived to be about sixteen years old. He was such a sweetheart. He got cancer in his back leg, and we had the cancer removed twice. It seemed to grow back faster each time. The veterinarian said he wouldn't operate again because it grew too quickly. We either had to get treatment or remove the leg.

Our concern was less stress for the dog, so I checked out what other vets had done. They showed me pictures of dogs that had received treatments. All the dogs were covered in sores for a long time after the treatment. They looked miserable. I asked the vets if each treatment was an additional cost, and the answer was always "yes," until it was thousands of dollars, and the dogs were still not healed and were miserable.

My vet had already told us that removing the leg wasn't hard on the dog. We returned to our vet and said, "Remove the leg." Tuffy 1 came through and had no problems. He jumped around and had another few years of a happy life. We were delighted with our decision.

My precious Tuffy passed while we went through the second and third companies. It usually takes a while to get over the loss of a pet. I missed my Tuffy so much! With the failure of the companies, the depression got worse. People told me to "just get over it," but unless you are experiencing depression, you have no idea how bad it can get.

We were playing cards with friends when they told me, "Just get over it."

The man was mentally abusive to his wife, and I thought, *I don't need to retake this and from this man.* I got up from the table and said to my husband, "I am ready to leave." They continued to say I needed to "just get over the depression," and I told my husband I wanted to leave. He looked stunned and didn't move. I told him I would walk if he didn't take me. It would have been a *long* walk. Everyone got up, and we left. If you have never been depressed like that, don't try to talk to someone else about depression. You have no idea. If we could "get over it," we would. It took me a while to feel comfortable with those friends again, but we finally got past the awkwardness.

Finally, I was ready to accept another pet and asked my youngest daughter and her kids to go with me to get another dog. When we all got in the car, I said to the kids, "Now you all know why you are along, right."

And they said, "No, Grandma Sandy."

So I told them it was "to make sure Grandma Sandy only brought one dog home." We always get rescue pets from places that save animals. My last puppy cost me one hundred seventy-five dollars. It is hard to believe that "rescued pets" cost that much.

The second Tuffy came into our world about three months after Tuffy 1 passed. Our pets add so much to our lives, as empty nesters and all the kids gone. They are like our children, and we treat them well. Tuffy 2 was from a shelter and was very timid and dirty. He was a mess. I had to get him groomed before taking him to a veterinarian. He was scared and would run out if we had the door open. It's a good thing both Sam and I were younger because we had to chase him through the neighborhood. Once, Sam even had to get the car because Tuffy 2 ran so far. Eventually, he didn't run away. He knew he "had it made" at our house!

People teased me about naming the second dog "Tuffy 2." When I got the third dog, they asked if it would be Tuffy 3!

When we went to Wisconsin to visit my daughter, we left Tuffy 2 in a pet hotel. It was part of our vet's office and close by. He was so upset that he chewed up his blanket and wouldn't eat. My youngest son in Tucson went over to try and get him to eat "people's food," but he wouldn't. The staff at the pet hotel got so worried that they took him to the vet. It got so bad that my husband and I left Wisconsin immediately and drove directly home. We got to Tucson just as the pet hotel opened and got Tuffy 2. He was so relieved to see us. My husband said he would never leave our dog at a pet hotel again, and we haven't.

Tuffy 2 lived for about fifteen years. Like all the dogs, he slept with us. People got to know Tuffy 2, and everyone mourned with us when he passed. They didn't know what to say when they came to the house because Tuffy 2 didn't answer the door. My niece offered to bury Tuffy 2 in their backyard because she knew how much I loved him. We accepted her offer. She has placed a statue and artificial flowers on his grave—from the flowers we take off the graves of my mom, dad, brother, niece, and nephew.

CHAPTER 22

Life Now

While my youngest son was still living with us, my husband worked in the yard and had the garage door open so he could get back in the house. He heard the garage door close and thought my son had left and closed the door. He also thought I hadn't come home from work. He was trapped outside. Or so he thought!

He tried to figure out how he was going to get back inside. He saw our doggy door and thought maybe he could crawl through that. Nope, that didn't work. Now my husband is not a large man, but he is not *that* small. We have a smaller dog! He tried several things that didn't work. He didn't know that my son and I were in the house. My son was watching television, and I was making supper. I had seen my husband working in the yard and wasn't aware of his predicament. He tried several things, all of which failed. He tried for over thirty minutes and finally took the doggy door panel off the house. The window was from the top to the bottom of the sliding glass door so he could walk through it. All at once, my husband was standing in the doorway between our bedroom and family room with a startled look.

He said, "What are you doing? Didn't you hear me trying to get in for thirty minutes?" Of course, we didn't! We had to listen to everything he had done to try and get in. My husband can tell good stories, and they can be hilarious. Trying to get in the doggy door was the best.

We also had another instance with the doggy door, but it was not so hilarious. My younger son needed someone to watch their dogs while they were out of town, and we were their last resort. I looked at my husband, and he said it was okay. He never said no; bless his heart. Now, these were not just dogs. They were *big* dogs. My son convinced me that they *could not* get through the doggy door! Remember this.

Off they all went, and everything was fine. Our Tuffy didn't care about the extra dogs because he was in the house, and they were *outside*! Night came. We are all in bed, sleeping. All at once, I wake to the sound of one of the dogs chewing on the screen door. He kept it up, and my teeth were gritting from the noise. Finally, I went into the family room to sleep. My husband slept through it.

The next day, we were eating, and I could smell dog. Upon looking up, two dogs were standing in our bedroom doorway. Big dogs! Dogs that were not supposed to get through the doggy door. We got them outside, and my teeth are gritting again.

My son called to say they were on their way home. It was the rainy season in Tucson, and it was raining like mad that day. He casually asks about his dogs. I cannot help but start telling him about the chewed screen and them getting through the doggy door. He must have realized his mother had hit her limits. They had meant to leave the dogs and get them after the rain. However, in the pouring rain, they stopped, picked up two soaking wet dogs, put them inside the truck with everyone else, and went home. I told him they didn't have to take the wet dogs right then, but he was insistent. I guess he knew his mother was at the end of her rope, and it wouldn't help to tie a knot.

My husband and I appear to have different timetables. We don't usually eat meals together. However, if I make a roast or something special, he will eat the first meal with me. The second meal that needs to be heated is whenever he is hungry. It is usually 7:00 p.m. when he is hungry, and we joke. "Is the restaurant open?" "Does the sign on the door say open?" When I first said that, he just looked at me.

After the first time I asked him, he now says, "Yes, the restaurant is open." I ask him if the meal is good, and he says, "Yes, I always tell the waitress it is good." I ask him if he always tips the waitress as I haven't seen one! Old age can be fun if you make it so.

He left the garage door open once, and I told him the car was gone. He almost flipped. Now he knows better because I tease him. It keeps his ticker going! Sometimes I have to tell him that I am teasing. I tease the kids, also. They will look at me and wonder until I say, "I'm teasing!"

I come by this naturally. My mom did the same thing to me once. She had gone to Hemet, California, to see her brother and wife. She called me and said she had car trouble on the way back. Could I come and get her? Oh, wow! I'm afraid to drive alone to Phoenix, Arizona, which is about ninety miles away, and she wants me to go halfway to California. Wanting to be a good daughter, I said, "Sure, I'd be there to pick her up." I hung up the phone and thought, *Now, what do I do?* She quickly called me back to say she was home and in the yard. Whew! My ticker was working overtime. My mom and I could joke with each other.

CHAPTER 23

Broke Leg, Muffin

When we were first married, I would tell my husband that I wanted something, and he would immediately think I wanted it right now. He would get nervous and figure out how we would afford it. I had to sit him down and say, "Look, I may want it but not right now, and I may never get it. Do you understand me?" He didn't understand that I looked at things and sometimes contemplated them for several years after deciding I wanted something. And then, I might decide I didn't want it after all. Now, he doesn't worry when I say I want something. Usually, by the time I finally decide, I have changed my mind several times and figured out where I will get the money or don't want it after all.

We were shopping the other day, and I said something weird and asked if I embarrassed him. He said, "Not anymore!" It made me laugh. We've been married for thirty years! My husband has had a beard our entire married life. I have never seen him without one.

I am eighty years old, and Sam is eighty-three. We have eight children as I write this book. He has four boys, and I have two boys and two girls. The eight kids have given us eighteen grandchildren, and the eighteen grandchildren have given us thirteen great-grandchildren. Another four more are in the oven. You can't get a happier family than that.

Sam and I have had several pets while married. I brought my first pet, a miniature purebred poodle that I called Gigi, from Wisconsin. It cost about one hundred and seventy-five dollars. After that, we always bought rescue dogs.

You have probably counted the dogs that Sam and I have had since our marriage. When we married, I had one dog, and my husband said we wouldn't get another when he passed. I said nothing! Each time the dog died, I would get so sad that I would finally say, "I need to get another pet." He didn't argue! That's how we ended up with three more dogs to date.

Our last little furball rescue cost one hundred seventy-five dollars. That was the same as my purebred. Muffin, not Tuffy 3, was a puppy when we got her, and people worried we would be sorry for getting a puppy. She was part Yorkie and so cute. We thought about it but figured we could handle a puppy! When Muffin got scared, she would run and hide under our bed. That was very easy for her to do as a puppy. As she grew, it became harder to do. Finally, she has to squeeze her tummy to get under the bed. She continued to do it. We anticipated the day when she could no longer squeeze under the bed. The day finally came when I cut off the space for her to get under the bed. She would go to the middle under the bed, and we couldn't get her out when we needed to take her for grooming. I had also put in wood flooring and didn't want her scratching the flooring scrunching to get under the bed.

Muffin started bringing stones in from the yard as a puppy. It happened every day. She would put the rocks on our pillows as if they were gifts. We couldn't figure out why she was doing this. Finally, someone told us that she was teething! It began to look like the backyard was in our bedroom. Eventually, she stopped. I guess the teeth were all in!

It wasn't long before we realized she was in her "terrible two's." She thought everything was a plaything. She was into everything. It was usually me who had to scold her. Then she would look to my husband for support. He usually comforted her, and I would have to make him believe I was angry with him. Muffin always looks to my husband for backup. She tips her head to look at him back over her shoulder, and he pets her. She also rolls her eyes—a typical woman.

We asked each other if we regretted getting a puppy, and the answer was a resounding no. We had fun watching Muffin grow up. If you have patience, you can deal with a puppy when you are elderly. Getting an older dog might be better for older people with little patience. They sometimes need rescuing more than the younger dogs.

Muffin loves ice cubes. When she hears the ice cube maker, she runs to the kitchen from wherever she is. She will take the ice cube and eat it where she is comfortable. That might be our bed, in the living room, wherever. Sometimes it melts because she hears the refrigerator door and thinks she is missing out on getting some of our food, and she drops the ice cube. Muffin is the only one who eats in our bed!

We are "Mommy" and "Daddy" to Muffin. If I say, "Where is Daddy?" she will look at me and know I am talking about Sam. I tried to get her to go and get Sam when I broke my leg and needed him, but I could never train her to do it!

If Muffin does something I want her to do, I will say, "Good girl." One time, Sam did something adorable and thoughtful, and I told him, "Good boy," without realizing what I was saying. He looked at me, and we both laughed. The next thing I know, he says to me, "Good girl." Yup, you get caught up in your pets. But they keep you young.

We have a maid who turns down the covers on the bed. She likes to sleep on the sheets instead of the blankets, so she pulls the covers back when I make the bed. "She" is our furry four-legged child who thinks she came from royalty. We must teach her to put chocolate on the pillows, but she might eat them, and she can't have chocolate, so that is out. She sleeps with us at night.

She knows when it is time for bed and keeps looking at us— are you going to bed yet? She also knows when it is time for me to nap—usually about 2:00 p.m. If I get up from my chair about that time and take off my glasses, she will run, get one of her toys in her mouth, and run to the bed. She beats me there. I think that dog can tell time! Muffin knows when it is time for her to eat and go to bed. It's time for her to eat at 1:15 p.m. and for *us* to go to bed at 10:00 p.m. The minute we say, "Going to bed," she runs, gets her toy, and is also ready for bed. She also knows the word "ham." That is what we feed her at about 1:15 p.m., her lunch!

Muffin gets three cookies at bedtime. If one gets under the covers, she can smell it and pulls the covers back. If she can't find it, she keeps trying to find it. She gets so excited that she jumps all over the bed. Sometimes I have to get out of bed and find the cookie to go back to sleep.

She will put a treat somewhere on the floor and leave it. She knows where it is and will move it back if we move it. I don't remember our male dogs licking their toys. Maybe only female animals "clean" their toys and think they are babies. It is cute to watch her "clean her babies" and carry them all over the house.

Muffin will *not* eat food out of her dish. She insists that my husband feed her by hand, and the pieces must be small. At about 1:15 p.m., she usually is fed five thin slices of ham. Sam has to tear it into small pieces. If we set the plate down, she will not touch it. Muffin waits for my husband to feed her. She lets my husband know when she is hungry by pawing the jar with her food. He puts about eight or ten dog food bites on the couch armrest, and she eats those and looks at him for more. I told you, she thinks she is royalty.

Even the Queen of England's Corgis doesn't get treated like that. The Queen has more than one Corgi, so the group would be called a pack, a pocket, a wiggle, or a rowdy! Just a little bit of additional information. If I kiss my husband, Muffin squeezes in. She wants a kiss and to become a part of the "love in." My sister asks, "And who raised her?" Of course, I must admit we did.

All our dogs had to have the last "word." They would always say, "Woof," no matter who spoke. It became quite a joke.

One night, Muffin came hurrying into the house, through the doggy door, and under the bed. I saw her out of the corner of my eye. It was three in the morning. I twisted around and fell on my right side, breaking my leg in several places. My husband heard me fall and asked if I was okay, and I said I thought I was. Try as I might, I couldn't get up. He finally came to help. Amazingly, I didn't feel pain but couldn't get up. He called the Fire Rescue, and they came and took me to the hospital. My husband followed.

They had fixed my leg up by the following day, and I was ready for my room. I don't remember anything after telling my husband I couldn't get up. It was a total blank until I woke up in the morning after surgery. I called the kids to say their mom was in the hospital, and they were upset that we hadn't contacted them before. They told me, "Anytime one of us went to the hospital, we were to call them no matter the day or night." We hadn't called because it was three in the morning, and they couldn't do anything anyway. They said that was "no excuse!" It kind of sounds like what a mother would say!

The nurses said I had broken my leg so badly that the doctor had to put it back together like a puzzle. It had screws, nuts, bolts, and every other rod you could imagine. When the kids got to the hospital, the nurses were ready to get me on my feet. I didn't want anyone to hear me scream, so I kicked them all out of the room until I was on my feet, but they had me so doped up that I didn't feel anything.

They transferred me to a rehab facility within a few days, where I walked and exercised. By then, it *was* hurting! I was hospitalized for about three to four days and then transferred to rehab. The rehab place was very nice. The food was delicious as they had a real chef on board.

My husband came to see me every day. When he moved to Tucson, he became a "cowboy," hat, boots, et cetera. He moved to Tucson well before I knew him. So I could hear him coming down the hall in his cowboy boots, and I would say, "Here comes my cowboy." He usually came about 11:00 a.m. when my rehab was over and over the lunch hour. If someone had left the day before and there was an extra meal, they would give it to him. He is a thin man and enjoyed every mouthful because it was so good.

He would bring me fresh clothes for the next few days, take the dirty clothes home, and wash them. There was always news on my four-legged, furry child, Muffin. He said Muffin couldn't figure out where I was. She would run all over the house looking for me. I asked him to put her on the telephone so she could hear my voice. He said she would listen and tip her head side to side, and when he put the phone down, she ran all over—again looking for me. Pets have been such a joy in our later years.

When I came home in the wheelchair, she was scared of the wheelchair. She's a very nervous little dog. Lightning, fireworks, or someone out in the yard gets her so scared. She will follow us around and sit in a corner or under the bed. She barks like crazy when someone comes but runs when we open the door—not what you would call the "best watchdog!" She does try her best.

I had given myself four weeks to rehab and recover, and the staff knew that. They worked with me, and in four weeks, I said goodbye. I still have problems, but I walk. I think of the men in my life and realize that my current husband is the only man who would have helped me. He made sure I had something to eat, washed dishes and clothes, and took care of me.

I have fallen several times because I don't have good depth perception. A step seems to be two inches when it's four inches, and I trip. I can fall downstairs, upstairs, you name it! Once, I looked up to see a man on a balcony and tripped *over* a sidewalk. Now that is an accomplishment. My fall cut a "Zorro" sign on my nose. It was noticeable, but not one person mentioned it, which I felt was very kind. Not even my stepsons, who love to tease me, said anything. I still have some of the marks.

As you grow older, you get very patient with your spouse. My husband came into the kitchen the other day, and the water was running in the sink. He asked me why. I didn't know why, so I told him I was watering the backyard. He said that wasn't good because it ran up the water bill.

My husband and his second son love to hunt. We don't eat the meat because I don't know how to cook it, so it doesn't taste good, but his son does. They eat everything they shoot. My husband and son like to get their kill mounted if it is a record for the books. My stepson has his all over the house. My husband has been limited to his den—by me. I'm not too fond of seeing heads of dead animals in all the rooms. My husband said he was running out of space, and I told him to put the next one on the ceiling. He didn't think that was a positive solution. He has one mule deer mounted, which is a record in Arizona.

I don't go hunting with them, but I enjoy the stories when they come home. They are like Laurel and Hardy. The jokes they played on each other were hilarious.

CHAPTER 24

Second Retirement and Mom

As time went on, my mom got older and needed more care. She stopped driving at eighty, and I would take her for groceries. After a while, she didn't want to go because it was hard to walk, and I would go alone.

I became a little bit of a caretaker. She called me one night and said she had fallen and the firefighters were coming to help her. I told her I would be right there and rushed over. I had just gone to school for a traffic ticket and was afraid I would get another for speeding. I was trying to go fast, but not to get another ticket!

Lights flashed when I arrived, and they took Mom to the hospital. I stayed with her, and they fixed up the wound in her head. The doctor said she needed someone to stay with her all night. I guess that was me.

I called my sister and told her what was happening, but I couldn't reach my brother in Coolidge, Arizona. The following day, I tried again to get my brother but couldn't contact him. Finally, I called for a welfare check, and they called back and said that he was sitting on his sofa but didn't come to the door. That scared me, and I told them to just get to him. They broke down the door and called back to say he had passed away.

That news was very unexpected because my brother was not ill. Now, I had to tell my mom, who was injured, and call his daughters and my sister. My husband and I finally reached his daughters, took the one up to Coolidge with us, and got things rolling there. One daughter lived out of state and had to drive to Tucson. The police wanted the door fixed before leaving, and my husband and I were miles away. My youngest son happened to be in Phoenix, close by, and could go down and repair the door.

My brother made prior arrangements for everything to be taken care of when he passed. He made arrangements for cremation and for the ashes to be sprinkled over water. Therefore, my mom had no idea where his remains were. I didn't realize her concerns until she told me, "Sandy, I don't know where your brother is."

Because she is religious, I told her, "Mom, he is in heaven." She seemed to accept that, but I said we would honor my brother with flowers at Daddy's gravesite. That seemed to satisfy her.

My mom couldn't go to the memorial because it was in Coolidge and she could not travel. My sister was in a wheelchair and could not travel either. I had to stay home with Mom! So someone would be at the memorial from my brother's family; my kids went up and covered for the rest of us. Mom wanted to meditate while the memorial was going on, which is what we did. She was so upset because he wasn't ill.

When we went to Daddy's gravesite to place the flowers, a hummingbird followed me from the car to the gravesite and hung over me as I placed the flowers. After that, hummingbirds meant that my brother was nearby.

My mom spent the last five years in and out of the hospital. She had problems with her legs, fell once, and hurt her head badly. Earlier, she was in the hospital with stomach problems. My sister was disabled, so I was taking care of my mom. When I went to the hospital to see her one day, the doctor called me outside her room. He said I should take her home because she was dying. The next thing, a nurse came to her room to discuss rehabilitation. That didn't make sense. Why should my mom go to rehab if she was dying?

I motioned for the nurse to come out of the room and asked her. Wow! Was she mad at the doctor? The nursing staff knew nothing of Mom's condition. I took Mom home, and we discussed what the doctor had said. Mom lived several years beyond the three months the doctor had given her. We told Mom she had shown that doctor that she would "go" when she was ready, not when he said.

My oldest daughter came from Wisconsin to see her grandmother if she passed. She stayed for several days and got to see my mom and visit with the family. Mom fooled them all. She didn't die!

There came a time when Mom was having trouble staying alone, and I was going back and forth between her home and ours. I spent nights with her. Sometimes, I had to be there several days in a row. My husband accepted that I needed to do it and waited for me to return. When I would go home for clean clothes, I would ask if he remembered me. He said he thought I was his wife! It brought us closer together. Mom was worried about my staying so much. She had to go into the hospital again, and when she came out, I told her that I thought it would be better if she moved in with us. She wasn't happy about it but agreed.

When Mom moved into our home, she was ninety-six. She was worried about our dog, Tuffy 2, still alive. I didn't know that she had been afraid of dogs since childhood. Tuffy loved Mom, followed her around, and looked out for Mom. Later, after seeing how much Tuffy loved her, she told me she would have gotten a dog for a companion and company had she known.

Mom lived with us for seven months until I pulled my back. I was in such pain that I could not take care of her. One night, crying from the pain, I called my daughter and said, "I need your help." She was there as soon as she could come. My daughter stayed for the weekend until she had to go back to work. Before she left, she helped get Mom into an assisted living home that I had found before she moved in with us. Mom lived in assisted living for one year until she had a medical issue that was not treatable. We moved her to a hospice. My sister was in the hospital, and Mom knew that. Mom lived for thirteen days without food or water—until she knew my sister was out of the hospital. That night, she passed. The doctor could not understand why my mom was still with us, but I knew she was waiting so my sister could be at her funeral.

My mom passed at ninety-eight. I don't like the word "died." It sounds like that was the end. I don't believe it is the end. I think we "pass" from earth to heaven. Mom had told me what she wanted to wear, where she wanted the service, and other things. It sure helped. My sister was supposed to be the executor of the will, but she was disabled and couldn't do it, so the position was up to me. My brother had passed a couple of years earlier.

My sister's two daughters helped me with the funeral arrangements. Because my sister couldn't walk to the gravesite, we decided not to have a viewing there. I had arranged for pallbearers, and I mentioned to my oldest son that there was nothing for them to do. My oldest son casually says, "Well, if you want me to, I can push Grandma around outside the chapel in the casket several times." He didn't mean this to be sarcastic. We knew Grandma was laughing in heaven. It took the sadness away for a little while.

When my mom passed, some people wanted us to have a yard sale to sell the things no one wanted. My mom had told me that relatives held a yard sale for my grandma's things, and they charged so much that the grandchildren couldn't afford any of Grandma's items. They went to people who didn't even know Grandma. I was one of the grandchildren that couldn't afford anything!

Mom was distraught with the way that went. I knew Mom wouldn't want her things sold at a yard sale and insisted it wouldn't happen. Anything not needed or that family members didn't want was given to the Gospel Rescue Mission. We gave them much furniture to share with the less fortunate, such as a sofa, a bedroom set, and many other items. They brought a truck and almost filled it. Not charging was very important because I could not afford things as a divorced mom and didn't want other people to go through what I did—if I could help it. The Gospel Rescue Mission is generous and doesn't charge for its items.

Our family believes we can and should talk to our loved ones who have passed. It is good therapy for us. So when I received a bill for Mom after she passed, I said, "Mom, you have to come back and pay this bill."

I imagined her saying, "*No* way! It's all yours now." We imagine Mom dancing with Dad as she loved to dance. She knows where my brother is now!

I don't remember ever crying at a funeral, as the people are in a much better place. They are no longer in pain if they were sick and in lots of pain.

CHAPTER 25

Football, Settling into Retirement

My husband and I finally retired for the second time. We returned to work for a few years after retiring the first time, either out of boredom or because we felt we needed to earn a bit more cushion for our later years.

My husband could now watch football whenever he wanted—Thursday, Saturday, or Sunday. If I wanted to be with him, I needed to "learn the game." Of course, the rules made no sense, and I asked my husband questions. Why did the players sometimes start at the twenty-yard line and now at the twenty-five-yard line? Or why was there only one quarterback on the field at a time? Why did they only use half of the field? Oh, many things didn't make sense to me. I know the people who understand football are laughing.

When he told me the rules, they still didn't make sense. I tend to talk back to the TV or yell at the players, "Run, run, run!" Sometimes, I'm sure my husband would rather I go to the other room, but he cheerfully lets me yell and comment.

Patrick Mahomes replaced the Kansas City Chiefs' regular quarterback when I started learning football. I had no idea the size of these men and called him my "little man." I thought he was well put together and that all quarterbacks were short. He played well and was just an ordinary man to me. So I liked him, and he was "my little man." Whenever he played, my husband would be sure to let me know but finally said, "You know he is over six feet, don't you?" Um, no, I didn't know that. I still call him "my little man." When you are a great-grandmother, you can do that. It is a sign that you like someone.

I just about had the rules in order when the pandemic hit, and they changed the rules for safety's sake. It started all over again, "Why, why, why?" And now, my husband couldn't answer some questions because he didn't know why!

There are a few pleasures I have in my old age. If the players missed the ball in an obvious mistake, my comment is "Dumb s—t."

I also used that statement when shows were on TV. For example, a man runs away from the top floor of a cruise ship and jumps off. Then he yells, "Help," as he hits the water. "I can't swim." Now he is a dumb s—t.

The last word got me in trouble in my late teens because it was my word of choice when I had a problem. It was my baby's first word. My baby was running around saying, "Sit, sit, sit, sit, sit." As the song goes, "It had to be me!" And I had to stop saying it. That word had to come out of my vocabulary.

When the COVID-19 pandemic hit, my husband and I stayed home because my husband had several health issues, and we didn't feel safe going out. The last time we went out was for my birthday on March 19, 2020. In April 2021, after being fully vaccinated, we started to go out again. My husband didn't cut his hair during that time. He looked like Willie Nelson! His kids took pictures of him because they had never seen him with such long hair.

Our children on both sides were healthy and not concerned about the pandemic, and they continued to go out as usual but stayed away from us to protect us. As soon as the vaccines were approved, we were vaccinated. We got the booster when it was available to us. We got the second vaccine just recently.

I know there is much controversy about the COVID-19 vaccinations, but my husband and I believe they are safe and needed, just like polio and other vaccinations.

Another thing you discover as you age is that your memory and hearing fade. You get up, go into another room, and don't know why! It happens all the time. But the funniest thing is when the hearing goes and you think you know what your spouse says. We talk along, one talking about one thing and the other talking about something different until we stop and say, "What are *you* talking about?" Sometimes the two different subjects are hilarious! Once, we talked about two other things and didn't know it. We stopped because the conversation was so weird that I couldn't even put what I thought he said in the book. It was X-rated! I could not repeat it in mixed company! Wait until you are there, and you will understand.

After years of being in a wheelchair, my sister was hospitalized and in rehab for several months. She finally was able to go home. The nurses had her sign a do not resuscitate (DNR) form before she left—it was her choice. She was not forced! My sister went home from the hospital with beginning dementia and a hiatal hernia. She was alert and talking when she got home. She went to sleep that night, and the hospice staff told my nieces that if they fed her or gave her liquids, it could affect the hiatal hernia and cause harm. If my sister woke up "agitated," as they called it, they gave her a pill. My sister never fully woke up and passed about two weeks later. She passed on February 22, 2022 (2/22/22). I believe that my sister did not have to die. Therefore, I have told my children and husband that I will not sign a DNR form. They know what I want.

On a happier note, all of the kids are doing great. I don't have to worry about them and their families. They will all do fine in the years to come. They all know how to work, play, and enjoy their families. They have indeed been a mother's pride and joy. Based on how we started after the divorce, the average person might not have been so lucky. Don't be afraid to start over. Happiness is on the horizon. All you must do is believe in yourself and put one foot in front of the other. It will happen!

My oldest son has a great job. His wife has a rental home real estate business where she buys a "fixer up" and then rents it out. She has several, even one in Wisconsin—the one my oldest daughter rents. The rentals will be their retirement income when my son retires in a few years.

My oldest daughter lives in Wisconsin and sees her father regularly. She has a good job and has been able to work from home since the pandemic. She loves it because her two dogs are there, and she can watch them. She posts videos and pictures on Facebook to see "her children."

My two sons have traveled to Wisconsin to see their father a few times in the past few years.

My ex keeps in touch with my oldest son in Tucson and my oldest daughter, who lives in Wisconsin. He doesn't try to stay in touch with the youngest two.

My youngest daughter started church schools at two different churches when her children began classes. She was very nervous about taking on this endeavor as she had never done something like this before. Everything had to comply with state certification. The classes were prekindergarten.

We are all proud of her as the need for more and more classes has become a great money source for the churches. The parents love the classes so much that she has students ready to sign up well before classes start. She started one school at the first church they attended, and she was the director and a teacher.

Eventually, a group of members started a new church. With the new church, they also needed a school. My daughter also built that school and is the director and a teacher at this school. They have many classes and add new ones yearly as enrollment grows. The income adds significantly to the church's finances.

My youngest son is much like my dad. He is an inventor and welder. He and his wife have built a large shop to make pool fencing for the many Tucson pools. He was busy during the pandemic because people found ways to stay home, and pools were a good choice. He builds other items using welding to diversify the business and keep it profitable. I can find things that need building or repair, and he is always willing. He built a trellis for my parties, where I gave out prizes, a dozen roses, and tiaras to winning team members living in Tucson. He and his wife have made a very profitable business in welding.

It is a joy to watch the children, grandchildren, and great-grand-children grow and become successful people.

CONCLUSION

If you have read this far, thank you. I hope you have enjoyed reading our life story and realize that you can do the same. You, too, can turn your life around and come back and have a wonderful, successful life after starting in an abusive relationship. I mentioned the kids' many successes, and I had to brag. I told their stories so you could realize what is possible if you give yourself a chance. You can take your life back. It might not be easy, but it is well worth it. I couldn't have accomplished all of this without believing in a higher power. I only have a high school education and one and a half years of college. I gained much knowledge to accomplish impossible projects, which put me farther ahead. Believe, and you can achieve.

By writing this book, I have relived our lives with loving honesty. It has given me the freedom to forgive. It lets you see how important it is to get out of an abusive relationship. It isn't my intent to make it look like I am making the abuser look terrible. I intend to show the actions to identify them and hopefully change your life.

For the abuser, I congratulate you for realizing your problems, wanting to change, and reading the entire book. Please get the help you need to have a wonderful life. Remember your first family if you remarry and have more children. Your first children don't want to remember you as a parent who abandoned them. Remember their birthdays, Christmas, graduations, weddings, and children's births. Get the children gifts so they remember you. If you live in another city, travel to see them. It is well worth your money. As their families grow and they have grandchildren, great-grandchildren also remember them. Make them feel as important as your new family. You will never be sorry you took the time you did. Treat both families the same. Your first family will remember and love you for it.

My husband and I have three great-grandchildren we haven't seen—two only once or twice and the third never. That is because, in two instances, the fathers are raising the children. We continue to love and remember them on their birthdays, Christmas, and graduations, putting money in our safe until we meet them. We hope that they will want to make contact when they are older. We have recently contacted one of them and are so thankful that the parents are willing to share with us.

A second one has recently graduated from high school, and we connected with him. He knows we loved him all those years and have put aside gifts. Unfortunately, he doesn't want to be part of our lives.

And for the abused, try not to talk against your ex in front of your children. They know what happened because they heard the fights and saw the bruises. Would you please help them to heal while you are recovering? If they need counseling, get it for yourself and them. I should have done that, but I was too young to realize we *all* needed it. Live the extraordinary life you deserve and help other abused women or men to do the same. Yes, I know of abused men! If you managed to get free, help others to do the same.

You must be alert as people will always try to control you. Control is how people mentally abuse and harass. It isn't only in relationships. It is also in the workplace. Two of my bosses were great at it.

Remember, whenever you do something, it is the right time. I'm eighty-one years old and writing this book, and it is the right time. As I write this book and dredge up memories, it is depressing, but it is necessary if it helps just one person to take hold of their life and get out of their hell. As I write of the sadness, it affects my days. I had nightmares reliving these issues. Writing this book has been a labor of love. It forced me to relive harrowing memories.

I have included pictures, my paintings, and some great family recipes for your enjoyment.

Look to the future and make it a great life!

Mom and I always laughed and said we should write a book about our lives because no one would believe it. Well, here is the book! Who knows? Someday it might be a movie!

PICTURES

Sandy, kids, and Mom about two years
after moving to Tucson, Arizona.

Sandy's Graduation Picture
June 4, 1970

To the right is a picture of the
house and barn that Daddy
built for us kids at Christmas
one year. Yes, those are real trees
behind the house and barn.

My maternal grandma and grandpa and the surviving children. My
mom is the only girl. She was the last one born and is front and center.
They came through Ellis Island, and my siblings and I knew all of
them, which is very unusual. They didn't have a bank account, and
my grandma would crochet around bills. When they passed, my mom
said she had to be very careful that they didn't throw out money!

Here is a picture of our childhood home. We took the picture when we returned to Wisconsin and visited Fisk around 2010.

Me, my sister, and my brother.

Fisk School
1955–1956
Grades 1–8
My brother is in the back to the teacher's right in a plaid shirt.

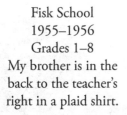

Our first Tuffy. He was such a sweetheart and a great protector.

Our Tuffy 2. Now you can see why we named him Tuffy 2.

"Her Royal Highness," our Muffin on the day we bought her. She was a rescue dog as were all the rest.

Our Muffin in today's time with her "toy" that she thinks is her "baby." She licks it as a mother would wash her child. She also grabs this when I say I am taking a nap at about 2:00 p.m., or she thinks it is time for bed around 9:30 p.m. She will look at us around these times and seems to say, "Well, when are you going to bed?"

My brother is in his policeman's uniform. He brought the kids and me to Tucson in late 1972.

My brother on his "pride and joy." He loved to go on motorcycle rides. He also had a pontoon boat that Mom liked to go on. He always said he was "spending his kid's inheritance."

Sandy's first Hawaiian trip
to Honolulu in 1992.

The famous blue taffeta dress!

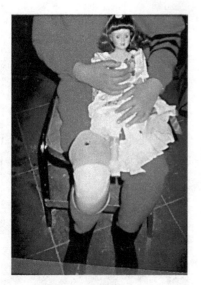

The doll with the artificial leg
was presented to a child in
Mexico. You can see it is the right
leg on both doll and child.

Christmas 1963, oldest daughter
playing her new piano.

Our oldest son's grandfather gave
him a calf to raise for showing at the
county fair. He sold the calf after
the fair and used the money to buy
himself a trumpet so he could be in
the band. He brought it to Tucson.

My oldest
daughter is a
"Bluebird" on
the left and after
"flying up" to
Camp Fire girl
on the right.

Hands Across America, Sunday, May 25, 1986.
My youngest daughter is third from the left.

Me on the day my oldest daughter got married. She wore my bridal gown and veil. She was so tiny that she had to have it taken in quite a bit! I was about forty-seven. She had been married at fourteen, but the marriage didn't last.

Four-generation picture. *Front row*: Mom and me. *Back row*: my oldest daughter on the right, and her daughter is on the left.

Pictures from our first date, December 12, 1987.

Acapulco, 1993.
We watched as the divers climbed
to the top of the cliff and then
saw them jump off. It was pretty
exciting as the ridge was so close.

Germany and Austria, 1996.
German cemeteries permit the burial of two to four urns
in the space needed for one casket. The people chose
cremation, which saves the expense of embalming.

Mozart's home in Austria, 1996. A red and white flag identifies the home. We could walk to the upstairs living area and see how he lived.

Alaskan cruise, 1999.
This was the first trip my husband was able to travel with me.
I earned enough trips so my mom could also go, and I paid for
Sam's mom to go out of my earnings from the company. Sam is
on the left, his mother, my mother, and me ready to board.

The wedding!
Our product line had a girl and a boy bunny named Flossie and Floyd. They were so popular that the company decided to add baby bunnies to the line for the next Christmas season. Kari An made the clothing for the bride and groom. We had to marry them before the company introduced the twins.

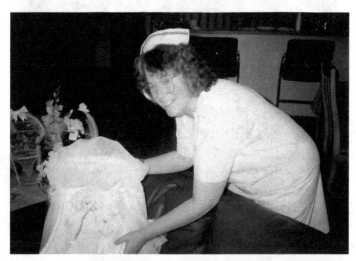

One of the newly born twins. We used every opportunity to have a "party!" Kari An made the babies' outfits.

All Paintings Are in Oil with a Palette Knife

RECIPES

The recipes are three of my favorites that are very easy to make, and I thought the readers of this book would love to try them. They are very old, and I have made them for the family for over fifty years. Enjoy!

Never Fail Piecrust

The ingredients sound weird, but this crust rolls out and browns beautifully. You will never have problems with piecrust again! (I remember my mom getting so frustrated trying to roll out the piecrust that she'd throw it on the table. We kids got quiet when that happened.)

1 lb shortening (2 cups)
1 tsp baking powder
2 tbs brown sugar
4 cups flour
2 tsp salt

Mix the above ingredients. Beat 1 egg in a measuring cup. <u>Add 1 tablespoon vinegar (yes) and enough water in a cup to make 3/4 cup liquid.</u> Add to the above dry ingredients. Makes enough crust for 4 double pies. It may be frozen or kept in the refrigerator for 2 weeks. You can roll it out immediately. No getting cold in the fridge first!

(Recipe is from Wisconsin and is over fifty years old in 2020. It is very flaky and easy to roll out. I don't know who gave me the recipe.)

Soft Sugar Cookies

(These cookies have less sugar and can be eaten by someone with diabetes if you don't frost them.)

3 1/4 cups sifted flour	1 egg, unbeaten
1 tsp soda	1 1/2 tsp vanilla or 1 tsp nutmeg
1/2 tsp salt	1 cup sugar
1/2 cup soft butter (use half butter and half shortening)	1/2 cup sour cream

Sift together flour, soda, and salt. Combine butter, sugar, egg, and flavoring in a large bowl mixer—cream for 2 minutes. Add sour cream and then flour mixture, and beat on low speed. Roll out on the floured surface to 1/4 inch thickness. Be sure not to roll them too thin. Sprinkle with sugar or frost.

Bake for 12 minutes at 350 degrees. Cool. Makes 2 1/2 dozen cookies. Do not frost the cookies if they are to be eaten by a person with diabetes. I double the recipe and must make them several days in a row as they are so good, and I give them out to family and friends.

(Recipe is from Wisconsin and is over fifty years old in 2020. I don't know who gave me the recipe.)

Cranberry Bread

(Recipe is from my sister-in-law in Wisconsin and is over fifty years old in 2020. The bread is delicious and very easy to make.)

2 cups flour	1 cup nuts, chopped (optional)
1 egg	2 tbs butter
2 1/2 tsp baking powder	1 tsp baking soda
1 cup cranberries, sliced	Juice and rind of 1 orange
1 cup sugar	1/2 tsp salt

Preheat the oven to 350 degrees. Add water to orange juice to make 3/4 cup of liquid. Mix all ingredients and pour into a greased loaf pan or make cupcakes. Bake for 30 minutes or until done. Cupcakes will take less time.

ABOUT THE AUTHOR

Sandra Fatovich, at eighty-one, wrote her first book, believing there is never only one time to do something important. She used her maiden name, Sandra L. Buehring, to honor her family, who helped get her life back. The book tells the story of her life from her happy childhood to her marriage to her high school sweetheart. Only then did she discover that he was controlling and abusive.

The book follows her thirteen years of marriage and, at thirty-one, her divorce, with four children—ages thirteen, twelve, eight, and one—to support alone. She moved to Tucson, Arizona, where her family lived, and they remade their lives.

Her goal in writing the book is to help others recognize an abuser and retrieve their lives.

Sandra continues to live in Tucson with her husband, Sam. They have been married for thirty-one years and have a total of eight children together—six boys and two girls. These eight children have given them eighteen grandchildren and thirteen great-grandchildren.

Today they are debt-free and enjoying retirement with their large family. Their beautiful home looks out at the Tucson mountains.

Printed in the USA
CPSIA information can be obtained
at www.ICGtesting.com
LVHW090346190924
791303LV00002B/247